Landscape Design in Chinese Gardens

"The essence of substance lies in emptiness, and motion originates from tranquility; herein resides the principle of garden creation."
— *Professor Chen Congzhou's painting with philosophical verses addressed to the author.*

Landscape Design in Chinese Gardens

Frances Ya-sing Tsu
(Zhu Ya-xin) *

*Associate Professor, Tongji University,
Shanghai, People's Republic of China*

* *Pinyin transliteration of the author's name,
under which she has published.*

McGraw-Hill Book Company

New York St. Louis San Francisco Auckland Bogotá Hamburg
London Madrid Mexico Milan Montreal New Delhi Panama
Paris São Paulo Singapore Sydney Tokyo Toronto

Library of Congress Cataloging-in-Publication Data

Tsu, Frances Ya-sing.
    Landscape design in Chinese gardens.

    Bibliography: p.
    Includes index.
    1. Gardens, Chinese.   2. Gardens — China.   3. Gardens —
Design.   4. Landscape architecture — China.   I. Title.
SB457.55.T78   1988   712'.0951   87-2837
ISBN 0-07-065339-9

1 2 3 4 5 6 7 8 9 0   HAL/HAL   8 9 2 1 0 9 8 7

ISBN 0-07-065339-9

The editors for this book were Nadine M. Post and Esther
Gelatt, the designer was Naomi Auerbach, and the production
supervisor was Dianne Walber. It was set in Garamond by
Progressive Typographers. The jacket was designed by the
author.

Printed and bound by Arcata Graphics/Halliday.

Contents

List of Famous Garden Plans

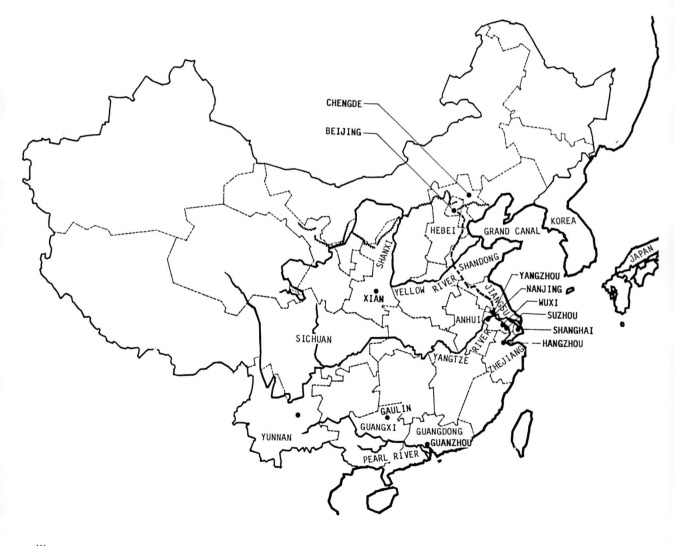

Preface

Books on the Chinese garden written in English are scarce; books on the Chinese garden emphasizing design are rare, even in Chinese. This book endeavors to fill the blank, and what triggered my interest in this project was the tremendous enthusiasm aroused in the audience during my lecture tour to Sydney University, Australia, in 1982. The response to the lectures I gave in the College of Architecture at the University of Nebraska — and encouragement from colleagues there — further impelled me to undertake this exciting and challenging project. With the background of architectural professor and designer, I try in this book not only to demonstrate the achievements of the Chinese garden through subjective appraisal, and emphasis on its historical origins, but to disclose and explain the underlying design principles, supported by plans, illustrative photos, and diagrams of celebrated gardens.

I am aiming at architects, landscape architects, designers, and students of these disciplines as the primary readers, but the book is also intended to enhance garden lovers enjoyment of Chinese gardens by showing them how to observe with "educated eyes." Also, I am attempting to arouse new interest in Chinese garden art.

As all architecture is built to fulfill physical and aesthetic needs of humankind, similarly the traditional Chinese garden — taken as a variety of architectural form — was intended as a living environment instead of a source of pleasure as in many other garden schools. I have endeavored through this book to promote the understanding of how a built environment might be greatly improved by a design process involving intimate cooperation between clients and designers. This procedure particularly involves continued efforts of the related parties after completion — owners and successive designers, for example — to achieve perfect architectural work. I have perceived that architecture and the profession of architects are not as well appreciated and recognized as most other fields of science or art; but since architecture is integrated with human life, I firmly believe it is possible and necessary to make architectural books comprehensible to all readers. This is especially true for garden design. If this book accomplishes a little in this respect, I will credit myself with having fulfilled the duty of an architect.

The book is in three parts, consisting of an introduction, 12 chapters, and an epilogue. Part One examines the unique characteristic of the Chinese garden in comparison with western garden tradition. Historical background and the garden evolution are organized in a succinct manner with an emphasis on design. Chinese gardens are classified geographically and also according to their original purposes, to clarify the diversified ways they are referred to in different books. The two major schools of oriental gardens, the Chinese garden and the Japanese garden, are compared as to their distinguishing characteristics and their historical affiliations.

The various components used in the Chinese garden are introduced in Part Two, with examples from famous gardens, illustrated with numerous photos of scenic details. Design process and general principles of spatial and scenic design, along with numerous illustrations, are presented in Part Three, Chapter 10. Chapters 11 and 12 explore the essence and methods of private gardens from an architect's viewpoint and are intended to serve as designers' reference on the creation of seeming spaciousness in a limited area. They also introduce ideas and methods for dynamic viewing, which I feel are valuable for the enrichment of environmental design in modern practice.

All the Chinese names in this book are transliterated according to the Pinyin system, the Phonetic Alphabet System with Mandarin, the nationally recognized modern Chinese pronunciation, to coincide with publications from China. Translations of the names are used in the text for the English-speaking reader, and names in Chinese are provided in the garden plan plates to denote the origins.

Three valuable Appendixes give plans of the various gardens, a chronological table of Chinese dynasties, and the names of the gardens in English translations and in Chinese.

Frances Ya-sing Tsu

Acknowledgments

First of all, I wish to acknowledge the contribution of my husband, Wong Chi-ching (Wang Ji-qing), for the revealing photographs he took to illustrate this book. Chi-ching is Professor of Architectural Acoustics at Tongji University; he is a very active acoustician in China. As an amateur photographer, he took the opportunity—when traveling around the scenic cities of China lecturing and consulting on acoustics—to use every bit of free time in his tight schedule to produce these beautiful photos of the illustrious gardens. Having worked together in our related fields for over 30 years, we once again cooperated exceedingly well on this book, and the experience was as wonderful as ever.

My greatest indebtedness is to the faculties and students of the architectural department, Tong-ji University, Shanghai, and the Nanjing Institute of Technology, Nanjing, who participated in surveying and drafting the traditional gardens at successive on-site workshops for architectural history classes. All these beautiful drawings, which I have used for preparing the illustrations, have become a treasure for the world to see in studying Chinese garden art. The plans of the gardens in this book were developed from these works of students supervised by the respective faculties.

I am also deeply indebted to the late Professor Liu Dun-zhen's *Classic Gardens in Suzhou,* 1982, Professor Chen Cong-zhou's *Dissertations On Chinese Gardens,"* 1982, and the late Professor Tong Jun's *Essentials of Garden Building History,* 1980, for important ideas on Chinese garden art which I have studied with respect. A number of articles in Chinese architectural journals—*Architectural Journal* and *Architects*—were most valuable reference sources.

I especially want to express my heartfelt thanks to Professor Chen Congzhou for his kind help in the preparation of this book. He generously supplied me with the latest articles of his resourceful dissertations on Chinese gardens, which much enlightened me. In fact, his lifelong devotion to research in Chinese traditional architecture and his encouragement of my desire to introduce Chinese architecture to the world became incentives for my writing this book.

I happily acknowledge my gratitude to Professor Robert F. Guenter for this generous assistance in Chapter 4, on Japanese gardens; to Kara Lynn Klarner and Susan Kaisand for reading the manuscript; and to Miao Pu for redrawing some of the illustrations.

Much gratitude is due to Professor W. Cecil Steward, dean of the College of Architecture, University of Nebraska-Lincoln, Professor Richard L. Austin, University of Nebraska-Lincoln, and Dr. Dean Hubbard, president of the Northwest State University of Missouri, for their assistance in many ways that made this book possible.

Last but not least, I wish to express my gratitude to all my American friends for their hearty encouragement and valuable advice, especially to Lillian and Wilfred J. Gregson. Their enthusiasm was most supportive to me, and Lillian kindly proofread the first manuscript.

PART ONE

Introduction

CHAPTER ONE

General View

The traditional Chinese garden is held in high esteem in the Chinese history of culture, art, and architecture. As a form of art, it arose from the fertility of ancient Chinese civilization, assembled and blended with the ideas and approaches of traditional Chinese painting and also intimately related to literature, poetry, music, and even drama. The style of the Chinese garden originated and developed over 3000 years and was valued as a living environment with naturalistic beauty, serving the sophisticated daily and sociopolitical needs of the ancient garden owners.

Physical Context

China is a country richly endowed with a diversity of magnificent natural landscape views that are beyond human imagination. Fascinating scenes of footless cordilleras floating on the clouds (fig. 1.1), grotesque aged pines, struggling for life upon the sparsely vegetated cliffs and stretching their branches over extraordinarily textured rocky peaks (fig. 1.2), frequently appear in celebrated Chinese landscape paintings. The subjects of these artworks might appear to be imaginative creations, but anyone who has toured among the fascinating ranges of scenic mountains in the vast territories of the country would vouch for their authenticity. One would deeply appreciate the beauty of motion expressed in landscape painting after witnessing the seething and emerging mist in Huang Shan, the Yellow Mountain, in person. Paintings of precipitously sculptured cliffs rising abruptly from the placid mirror-like river Li Jiang, in the city of Guilin, Guangxi Province, and the grotesque posture and fabulous texture of the natural rocks in Shi Lin, the Stone Forest,

FIG. 1.1 *Scenic Huang Shan, Yellow Mountain, Anhui Province.*

in Yunnan Province (fig. 1.3), might also seem incredible if enchanted photojournalists had not repeatedly introduced these scenes to the world.

A visit to the picturesque lake Tai Hu, the Grand Lake, in Jiangsu Province, would also convince one that Chinese gardens are accurate in representing the general atmosphere of the natural landscape as well as the detailed designs, such as the rockery girdling the garden ponds that was constructed to imitate the shores of natural lakes. Thus, the abundance of natural landscape resources originated and nurtures both Chinese garden scenes and Chinese landscape paintings.

Conceptual Idea

According to ancient Chinese tradition, the human character could be partly judged by the quality of its response to nature. A person who truly loved

mountains and water more than worldly interests was accepted as a person of deep spiritual cultivation. Painters and poets, wandering among the mountains and rivers, created paintings of varied styles depicting the magnificent landscape scenes and composed verses expressing their admiration for the beauty of nature and their tendency to renounce mundane thoughts. All these activities not only lent success to their artistic accomplishments but also entitled them to be referred to as people of higher interests and purified minds.

Nature is loved and held in highest honor, but this does not mean that objects of nature have to be presented in their original form. The main principle of Chinese painting, also adopted in Chinese garden art, is to depict nature's beauty — not with a naïve imitation of realism but by recreating the essence of nature. The goal is to present nature in a lyrical and artistically succinct manner; that is, naturalness enhanced by artificial effect.

The Chinese painter's approach to artistic creativity is very different from

FIG. 1.2 *The Huang Shan pine, welcoming guests with its outstretched branches.*

FIG. 1.3 *Shi Lin, the Stone Forest, Yunnan Province.*

that of the western tradition. The occidental tradition is to paint according to live objects. Chinese landscape painters base their artistic presentation on traveling widely in the mountains and waters; they learn the essence of nature by heart.

Unlike modern western painting, which tends to stress the physical beauty of forms, color, and light — giving strong stimulation to the visual sense — the Chinese traditional landscape painting strives for the beauty of the conceptual idea, using visual objects to present the fascinating atmosphere existing in natural landscape. That is, the goal is to express the mood and the spirit observed in nature and the emotion or the morality inspired. The ultimate expectation is to arouse the observer's sympathetic response. Likewise, ancient Chinese garden makers composed picturesque landscape scenes, hyperbolizing the impression they obtained from nature in accordance with their own ideal. The thought-provoking intention, unique to Chinese landscaping, is absent in occidental practice. Chinese artistic creations are intended to be from nature, exalting nature, and inspired by nature — but with a subjective concept. During long centuries, Chinese landscaping was achieved by naturalistic, idealistic, and symbolic means, not only with artistic principles but also with philosophical ideas.

Since Chinese gardens are closely related to traditional Chinese painting, it is most helpful to know both the methodology and the aesthetic conceptions of traditional painting in order to better understand the Chinese garden. Traditional Chinese painting, particularly, denounces the photographic way of depicting form with form and demands depiction of spirit with form. Although the form of the object is respected, distillation, exaggeration, and deformation are allowed.

Xieyi, which means depicting the sentiments, is the fundamental approach shared by all forms of Chinese visual art. It constitutes an aesthetic conception entirely different from the realistic tradition of occidental art. Chinese art has passed through a long process of evolution since originating as realism. For more than a thousand years, Chinese artists have not been content to limit their work to the bounds set by reality. Gu Kaizhi, a painter who lived A.D. 346–407, was the first to express this as a theory known as "using the form to show the spirit." Vivid rendition of the spirit was valued more highly than fidelity to the object in form. Later, guided by the theory that "likeness in spirit resides in unlikeness," highly artistic forms developed with "ambiguous likeness."

According to these rules, the presentation of garden scenes is to grasp the essence of natural landscape. Re-creation is based on profound observation that concentrates on beauty and discards the redundant. In this sense, Chinese garden making is a process of abstraction and stylization based on reality. The designers present not only what they see and feel but what they imagine, on the basis of what they saw. Nurtured by important theories of Chinese visual artistic creation, such as "take nature as one's teacher and the heart as a source of inspiration" and "manifest the imagination to depict the marvelous," Chinese garden art flourished side by side with Chinese painting.

Being juxtaposed with *xieyi, gongbi* is the other major type of Chinese traditional painting. Paintings of *xieyi* type are marked by exaggeration of form and the liberal and bold use of ink and strokes. The *gongbi,* which means meticulous brushwork, is characterized by strict and detailed representation of the subject.

As far as color is concerned, monochrome Chinese ink is considered even more distinctive than multicolor. Concentrating on changes of tone, artists could focus all their attention on expressing their special feelings and ideals or visualizing a particular atmosphere through a certain subject. Monochrome paintings are also greatly enhanced by highlighting with very simple and faint

FIG. 1.4 (top left) *Summer-Retreating Mountain Villa, Chengde, Hebei Province.*

FIG. 1.5 (bottom left) *Behai Gongyuan, the North Sea Park, Beijing.*

FIG. 1.6 (top right) *Jixiao Shanzhuang, the Roar-Resounding Mountain Villa, Yangzhou. Looking from the "balcony," the two-story walking gallery, onto the stage pavilion.*

FIG. 1.7 (bottom right) *Zhuozheng, Yuan, the Unsuccessful Politician's Garden, Suzhou, viewing from Willow-Shaded Winding Path toward Leaning Jade Studio (plan 1).*

but sophisticated use of pigments. As a contrast to *xieyi,* the most elaborate works of *gongbi* paintings were presented in multichrome, and even the color gold is introduced.

Having been introduced to the different schools of Chinese painting, one would naturally associate the private gardens with a subtle version of *xieyi* painting in monochrome while considering the imperial gardens as gorgeous *gongbi* painting in gilded multichrome.

The old-school critics, both oriental and occidental, maintained that only a good painter could design a good garden. A Tang dynasty poet painter, Wang Wei (A.D. 701–761), was highly praised for "his poetry, picturesque; his painting, poetic." Possessing "the poet's feeling and the painter's eyes," he designed his own garden to enrich his years of retirement. Wang Wei's garden, Wang Chuan Bie Ye, Villa Along Rimlike River, was repeatedly praised and idealized as the best garden ever built in Chinese history.

Functional Aspects

It is essential to point out that the terms *Chinese garden* and *Chinese garden design* should not be taken as equivalent to the contemporary conception of "landscape architecture" or "landscape design." Landscape design and landscape architecture often serve as a foil to architecture even when it encompasses a city.

The existing private gardens were built as retreats by gentlemen scholars, the rich and ranked class of feudal society. Most of the private gardens were built adjacent to their city residences, as an extension of the formal courtyard houses, to provide a refuge from the tension of the hierarchical society. Some were constructed as resorts intended only for occasional visits, when house gardens were considered too familiar to lend enchantment. The original motive for building private gardens seems to have been an admiration for wilderness hampered by unwillingness to forsake the convenience of city life. Efforts were made to create miniature worlds of wilderness in city areas.

Private gardens were intended to offer ideal environments for scholastic activities such as studying, painting, composing verses, cultivating plants, fish, and birds, and garden making itself. In many of these gardens, China's great poets and painters met and achieved their splendid works. Thus, Chinese gardens have served as an important background for Chinese civilization.

The earliest imperial gardens were large tracts of land preserved for hunting. Later imperial gardens were built by ancient emperors for the pursuit of secluded life embraced by the beauty of nature. As they were limited by participation in political obligations, they arrived at the solution of constructing gardens of enormous scale that included duplicated imperial court and residential palaces. They also reproduced the finest scenic landscape views to be found in their territories. Therefore, Chinese gardens, private and imperial, drastically limited in area or with vast expanses of land use, are all cosmic diagrams that reveal a profound and ancient view of nature, incorporating the individual garden maker's world view and lifestyle.

In China's past, garden owners strove to make their garden look scholarly and refined. Gardens were celebrated for their tastefulness not for their opulence. Even the ancient emperors, in spite of all the luxuries provided in their magnificent palaces, admired the life of country poets, painters, and recluses and strove to seek a place for physical and spiritual refreshment. The Summer-Retreating Mountain Villa in Chengde, Hebei Province, provided this respite through its touch of rusticity (fig 1.4), which apparently deviated from such palacial expressions as that of the Summer Palace and Beihai Park (fig. 1.5).

Suzhou in Jiangsu Province is famous as the "city of gardens." Gardens in Suzhou, celebrated as embracing the essence of Chinese garden art, are nurtured by their literate owner builders' mastery of culture and art. The gardens in Yangzhou, built mostly by prosperous merchants, were used more as places for holding parties, entertaining friends, and other social purposes than as secluded retreats for self-cultivation such as the Suzhou gardens. Thus, space and scenes in Yangzhou gardens were relatively concentrated, disclosed in a more open manner, and embellished with extensions of distinctive rockeries. More sizable buildings were erected to cope with the congregation of participants. Stages were even included—for music or theatrical performances. These gardens, as a sign of conspicuous consumption, served to display the wealth of their owners, as well as demonstrating the owners' artistic cultivation. As a whole, the Yangzhou gardens (fig 1.6) seem to seek instant impression, which distinguishes them from the more dainty and subtle presentations in Suzhou gardens (fig. 1.7). Therefore, as all art is deeply and intimately connected with daily needs of human life, the Chinese garden is particularly demonstrative, being a vital living environment.

CHAPTER TWO

Historical Perspective

Historical Background

During more than 3000 years of antiquity in China, totalitarian emperors reigned until the fall of the latest Qing dynasty in 1911. The persistent domination of feudalism was consistent with the teaching of the most influential Chinese philosopher, Confucius, who lived 2500 years ago. Confucius taught the ethical importance of ritual in political and private life and greatly influenced all aspects of Chinese culture. Confucianism retained its constant importance within feudal society as an essential part of the ruling mechanism in spite of all the peasant upheavals and changes of dynasty. Detailed disciplines demanded the people's blind loyalty to the emperor, who was recognized as the divine ruler, the son of heaven. The fundamental unit of feudalism was the extended family, in which reverence and absolute obedience to the patriarch was demanded. Loyalty to the emperor and filial obedience to the patriarch were the basic tenets of Confucianism.

Confucianism—with its rigid and hierarchical conception of social organization—also dominated and strictly regulated the traditional architecture of China. The goal was an imposition of efficiency through the physical surroundings. This resulted subsequently in extremely restricted, formal, axial, symmetrical architectural layout of towns, temples, palaces, and residential courtyard houses. Thus, buildings for all purposes shared a basically stereotyped layout, differing only in size, dimension, and ornamentation ac-

I

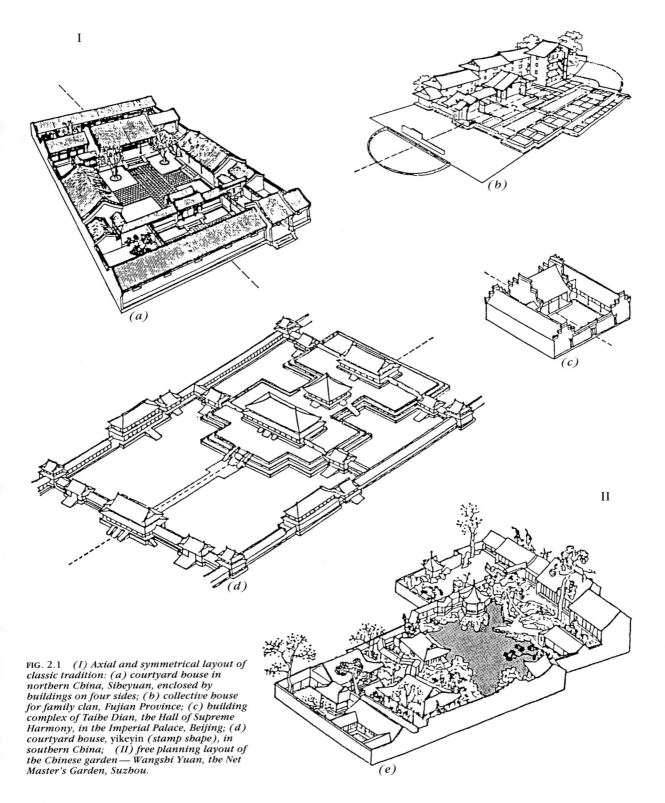

II

FIG. 2.1 *(I) Axial and symmetrical layout of classic tradition: (a) courtyard house in northern China, Siheyuan, enclosed by buildings on four sides; (b) collective house for family clan, Fujian Province; (c) building complex of Taihe Dian, the Hall of Supreme Harmony, in the Imperial Palace, Beijing; (d) courtyard house, yikeyin (stamp shape), in southern China; (II) free planning layout of the Chinese garden — Wangshi Yuan, the Net Master's Garden, Suzhou.*

(a)

(b)

(c)

(d)

(e)

cording to their functional needs (fig. 2.1). All buildings were ultimately regulated by the rank and social status of the occupants in the feudal society.

Even the use of utensils and clothing was under restrictions, starting as early as the Zhou dynasty, nearly 3000 years ago. People began to tire of the overdetailed regulations. During the long, disastrous period in ancient Chinese history called the Warring States (475–221 B.C.), successive tumult from the changes of dynasties led people to the trend of escaping from reality and their distressed state of mind. Consequently, the other great school of ancient Chinese philosophy, Taoism, came into vogue.

Taoism summoned people back to nature. Laozi, the supposed founder of Taoism, had greatly influenced the Chinese garden by censuring mundane interests and by exhibiting an immense love for nature. The Taoist ideal of beauty is expressed in asymmetry, with a curvilinear layout derived from nature and strikingly rebellious to the formal architectural tradition. The Chinese garden is, in fact, another Chinese architectural system, one that contrasts with the formal axial and symmetrical system of classical architecture. Seen in its special historical context, it was a unique form of revolution. Being given the title of garden, its spatial and architectural design were set free from official restrictions for buildings and thus lent the possibility of accommodating a more refreshing lifestyle for the ancient garden owners, including the reigning emperors. In this way, Chinese garden art had reached an apogee of original designing principles and methods.

During the long history of the Chinese garden, the Qin Han (221 B.C.–A.D. 220), Tang Song (618–1279), and Ming Qing dynasties (1368–1911) are the more important episodes of development. Like the architectural styles of the times, the Tang dynasty was characterized by a beauty of simplicity and conciseness, the Song and earlier Ming excelled in maturity, and the late Ming and Qing dynasties gradually inclined toward pretentious, elaborate embellishment. According to historical records, only a few of the distinguished gardens that had been repeatedly praised and depicted by Chinese classic literature and antique paintings were preserved. So many exquisite gardens were devastated or totally destroyed due to the natural calamities that occur over a long period in history and with all the successive warfare in the changing of dynasties in ancient China.

During the European invasions of the last hundred years, especially, none of the resplendent imperial gardens that took generations to elaborate escaped from being burned and looted. Among these, the Summer Palace (plan 14-1A) and Beihai Park (plan 15) have been restored to their original magnificence and opened to the public as parks. The Summer-Retreating Mountain Villa (plan 17) in Chengde, Hebei Province, which is the largest imperial garden in China and a rare example of a garden with natural landscape settings, is now under restoration. Yuanming Yuan, Garden of Perfect Brightness (plan 16), was the most imposing and beautiful imperial garden of the Qing Dynasty. It consisted of three subdivided gardens, Yuanming Yuan, Changchun Yuan, Lasting-Spring Garden, and Qichun Yuan, Gorgeous Spring Garden (plan 16). Celebrated as the "garden of gardens," this extensive and fabulous garden was built over a period of 63 years, beginning in

FIG. 2.2 *The ruins of Yuanming Yuan, Garden of Perfect Brightness, Beijing.*

1709. It was first completely destroyed in 1860 by invading Anglo-French forces. Shortly after partial restoration, the garden was again looted and burned by an army of eight allied western powers in 1900. Only a few ruins of the once exuberant baroque-influenced architecture, left in northwestern suburbs of Beijing, bear witness to its existence (fig. 2.2). Recently, an ambitious plan for restoring the garden was made. Restoration has been partially completed, but an enormous effort will be required before the garden's magnificence is finally presented in toto.

Extensive research has disclosed that in most of the surviving ancient gardens, only the general layout and certain pieces of rockeries, individual buildings or plants remain after successive deformation and reconstruction during China's long history. The classic gardens existing in China today were mostly newly built or reformed, with a more elaborate and decorative style, in the late Ming or Qing dynasties.

Since the fall of the latest dynasty, Qing, extensive garden building had come to a halt, due to continuous national warfare, economic depression, and the upper class's interest in western civilization. The gardens, both imperial and private, began to disintegrate under ill use and negligence. Since 1949, most of the surviving traditional gardens have been excavated and restored to their original magnificence in an effort at cultural preservation.

Compared to the number of highly esteemed gardens recorded in history, these gardens are but a token and cannot fully represent the multifarious styles and proclivities that flourished in different stages of the Chinese garden's historical evolution.

Neither the profession of architect nor garden designer existed in ancient China, despite all the ingenious work that had been accomplished. The garden makers were mostly the owners, themselves, who were highly cultivated in different forms of art. Others, such as scholars, painters, and poets—

sheltered under the roofs of their rich patrons — repaid their patrons by assisting in artistic or literary activities, by acting as consultants or secretaries in sociopolitical affairs, by teaching in the family school, and by helping in the planning of garden design and construction. Thus, the ancient Chinese gardens were not designed in a scientific, systematized manner. Rather, planning was guided by artistic considerations. As time passed, through sharing theory and principles with landscape painting — and guided by the gradually maturing techniques — famous garden makers emerged and Chinese garden art flourished.

Later, in the Ming dynasty, *Yuan Ye,* or *Garden Building,* the best ancient Chinese garden treatise for completeness and classified methods, was compiled in 1631 by Ji Cheng (Chi Cheng). He was a painter and rockery artisan who had become one of the most famous garden builders in Chinese history. *Yuan Ye* was introduced to the world by Japanese garden circles over 50 years ago. The Japanese translation of the book bears a remarkable title, *Excelling the Heavenly Creation;* it was honored as the earliest masterpiece of garden books. It is a feat of garden art, tracing the practice of garden making through centuries in ancient China. *Yuan Ye* provides a comprehensive survey, including the basic idea, general layout, design methods, and components of the garden with distinctive national characteristics. In spite of all the detailed instructions covered in the book, it is emphasized in the summarizing chapter that a garden is not constituted by any regulating rules but is an expression of nature's pulsating life. The book also asserts that since gardens are intended to appear natural — reproducing the charm of wilderness — it is necessary for any principles to remain elastic. *Yuan Ye,* which was written in an ancient Chinese literary style, was translated into modern Chinese and published in 1981.

Historical Evolution

The evolution of Chinese garden history in terms of reproducing the natural landscape can be divided into three episodes, each with a distinctively different approach (fig. 2.3).

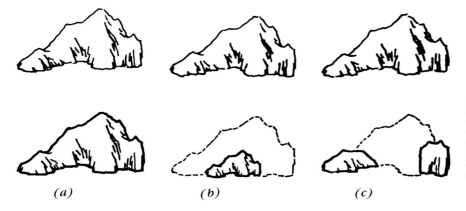

(a)   *(b)*   *(c)*

FIG. 2.3 *Three episodes of Chinese garden history in reproducing the natural landscape: (a) full-sized imitation; (b) miniaturization; (c) accessible segmental reproduction.*

An important garden construction recorded in ancient Chinese history is the Chang Chi, the Long Pond, built by Qin Shi Huang, First Emperor of Qin Dynasty (221–206 B.C.), with a large extension measuring 200 *li* east to west and 20 *li* north to south. (A single modern Chinese *li* equals 500 meters, but the ancient Chinese dimensional measurement is believed to be smaller than the modern *li*). This enormous, labor-consuming construction included the introduction of water from the river Wei He to fill the gigantic pond. The legendary island Penglai Mountain, supposed to be the magical dwelling of the immortals, was constructed with soil excavated from the pond. Later, the Emperor Wu of the Han dynasty (206 B.C.–A.D. 220) constructed the Taiyi Chi, the Grand Fluid Pond, embracing three legendary immortal mountains: Penglai, Fangzhang, and Yingzhou. This pattern of "three islands in a pond" was repeated in other gardens with varied designs and modified versions.

During this period, landscape gardens were basically full-sized reproductions of natural mountain and water scenes. This type of garden style, continued in ancient China, was believed to have started from the Spring and Autumn Period (770–476 B.C.), and came into vogue during the Qin and Han dynasties. The slave and feudal society afforded an immense supply of manual labor, which made possible the incredible, extensive earthwork of the imperial gardens. Stressing precision in reproducing natural landscape scenes, it was a purely naturalistic approach.

During the long, disastrous period of the Warring States (475–221 B.C.), the tumult of successively changing dynasties created a desire to escape from reality, from a distressed state of mind. Besides, the Taoist influence toward going back to nature, and the prevailing attraction to the wilderness of natural landscape scenes, made the admiration for gardens so widespread that garden construction was no longer limited to imperial enjoyment. Private gardens were built by bureaucrats and wealthy men of letters, so-called gentlemen scholars. The size of private gardens was limited not only by building cost but also by the hierarchical regulations of the feudal society molded by Confucianism. Nothing should surpass the imperial possessions in any way, including the size of a garden. Some ambitious bureaucrats did, however, venture to build gardens on a scale competing with imperial gardens. They were ultimately accused of violating the hierarchical order of the feudal society and being offensive to the emperors' absolute authority. Gardens were confiscated and the owners condemned. After that, private garden makers were wise enough to restrict their gardens to medium or small size.

The early private gardens were basically diminished imitations of the palatial gardens. Due to the drastic curtailment of area and the influence of the contemporary evolution of landscape painting, a new garden style began to surface after the Sui (581–618) and Tang dynasties (618–907).

During the Song dynasty (960–1279), landscape painting began to flourish as an independent school of fine art. It was recorded that celebrated paintings at that time depicted "a height of 8000 feet within 3 inches" in vertical compositions and "hundreds of miles within several feet" in horizontal compositions. At the same time, the new theory of landscape painting evolved, calling for a vivid presentation of the emotional expression in landscape painting that

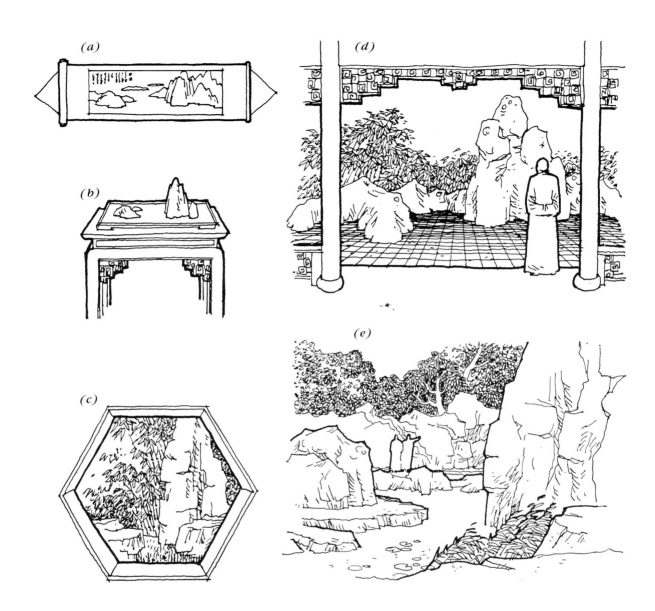

FIG. 2.4 *Different ways of reproducing natural landscape in the Chinese garden: (a) painting; (b) potted landscape; (c) window scene; (d) rock-plant composition in courtyard; (e) accessible artificial hill.*

would arouse the observer's imagination and response. This way of "depicting the feelings"—in opposition to the school of "depicting the reality"—had greatly influenced Chinese garden art. Thus, the processes of "shifting the universe and shrinking the land" and "enclosing the vastness of a hundred miles" were adopted in the Chinese garden through romantic imagination—by means of exaggerated symbolism with an emphasis on the expression of feelings, as well as the depiction of realistic details.

The teaching of Taoism stressed the absolute liberty of the spirit and sought to unify the subjective world with the objective world. When the vastness of nature is embraced by the mind, according to Taoism, one will be able to

perceive "vastness through miniature" or "small as large." For example, a profound love and an extensive experience of traveling in wilderness might enable one to perceive a small pebble as a large knoll, or a mere crack in a rock as a grand ravine sequentially suggesting the grandeur of a mountain range. Thus, with the natural mountains as a pattern, gardens were built as small worlds of fantasy and subsequently legendary immortal mountains were introduced in diminished versions. A small garden, with a miniature landscape scene, could be intoxicating and yet simple and inexpensive to construct. During this period, the evolution of garden art theory, the accumulation of technique in structuring the physical environment, and the introduction of subjective expression were essential in the creation of a new garden style.

The garden term *artificial hill* first appeared in poetry during the mid and late Tang dynasty. Gardens with miniaturized landscape were popular during the Tang dynasty and prevailed throughout the Ming and Qing dynasties. The essence of this style is the approach of "perceiving vast through miniature," but its fatal deficiency is being not accessible and good only for viewing. It does not achieve the ultimate goal of the Chinese garden, which is to create a viewable, tourable, and livable naturalistic environment.

Hence, the third episode of garden-building history appeared with the fall of the Ming dynasty. A garden master, Zhang Nanwei, advocated a constructed naturalistic environment accessible to human scale. His innovative approach was based on the fact that adventurous tourists exploring a real mountain range experience only segmental scenes of the mountain in succession. As for the entire picture of the mountain, they have to piece together by imagination

FIG. 2.5 (far left) *A medium-sized courtyard in front of a studio, adorned with an elegant rock-plant composition for static viewing; in Wangshi Yuan, the Net Master's Garden, Suzhou.*

FIG. 2.6 (left) *Artificial hill, modest in height, providing accessible touring paths with a variety of interest.*

FIG. 2.7 (below) *A footpath built of artistically arranged rocks provides the enjoyment of touring in the wilderness; in Canglang Ting, the Surging-Wave Pavilion, Suzhou.*

accumulated impressions of the fragmentary views they have observed. Chang Nanwei's theory coincides with a well-stated Chinese parable: "A leopard is recognizable by a pattern of spots on his skin." Artificial hills were built with a general appearance rather different from real mountains, but "seeing entity through detail" was expected. It resembles the Chinese way of "depicting a dragon by presenting a scale or a claw." The observer's imagination is provoked to visualize an entire dragon.

In reality, the panoramic view of a real mountain is only to be observed from a distance. This kind of pleasure could as well be supplied by other garden scenes in diminished scale, which are inaccessible but satisfactory for distant viewing. Therefore, the methods of both miniaturizing landscape (fig. 2.4*(d)*, 2.5) and reproducing segments of accessible landscape scenes (fig 2.4*(e)*, 2.6, 2.7) are practiced in existing Chinese gardens.

A crooked waterfront embankment, an undulating hillside, or a meandering footpath lined with ornamental rocks half screened by plants were structured in human scale. The general appearance of these rock compositions might not precisely resemble real mountains, but it would be artistic enough for viewing pleasure and realistic enough to provoke the image of touring through an extensive range of mountains.

This garden-building method is neither the primitive way of reproducing the entire mountain in full size and scale nor the presentation of a miniatured landscape intended to be viewed only from a distance as a "three-dimensional painting." In theory and practice, this school is acclaimed for its innovative style and original approach. It also marked the ultimate maturity of ancient Chinese garden art.

In conclusion, the art of ancient Chinese garden design could be divided into three episodes with three different schools of approach, each with its own naturalistic, romantic, and realistic trend. In fact, three schools emerged successively and were practiced in overlapping time sequence or found existing simultaneously within a single garden.

CHAPTER THREE

Comparison of the Chinese and European Garden

Differences

The Chinese garden differs substantially in content from gardens in the rest of the world. Gardens in the western tradition are a product of leisure, serving no immediate practical purpose, while the Chinese traditional garden is a microcosm for living. A western garden, classic or naturalistic, is the link between people and the world in which plant material is used as the major component, while a Chinese garden is a built environment of livable spaces with natural and artificial components to fulfill physical and spiritual human needs. In other words, Chinese gardens were built for habitation as well as for pleasure. Therefore, the exceedingly high density of architecture dominating most of the Chinese private gardens — and the major scenic sections of the imperial gardens — are inconceivable in any other type of garden in the world.

The Chinese naturalistic garden and the European geometrical garden are the world's two major ancient garden systems. The ancient western gardens, with a layout based on a rectilinear tradition, can be traced back to Egyptian and Islamic influence. The Renaissance Italian and French gardens are planned in axial and symmetrical layout with series of geometrically shaped parterres and rectilinear paths, assimilating a spatial structure of rooms and corridors in architectural design. Geometrical gardens of the west present a strong artificially created order in opposition to nature, human power expressed by organizing nature under the control of human will.

Classic gardens of western tradition were built around edifices with garden architecture consisting of terraces, parterres, fountains, flights of stairs, railings, and retaining walls. Architectural features — a trellis, an open gallery, a pavilion, or a small garden house — are found in extended landscape gardens, dispersed in the planted landscape; they usually serve as ornaments rather than lending themselves to a practical function such as a rest stop. The garden sets off the edifice; it becomes the approach or the background for the ornamental architectural features.

The English landscape garden, contrastingly lyrical in layout, concentrates more on faithful reproduction of natural landscape scenes. In order to make the garden as close to nature as possible, larger tracts of land are acquired so that the expanse of grass meadow with undulating land forms will manifest its magnificence. In so absolute a naturalistic tendency, a small garden house would most likely be hidden as being incongruent with the naturalistic style.

The Chinese garden belongs to an entirely different school of thought, compatible with ancient Chinese philosophy: It is a profound expression of Taoist natural philosophy. The ancient Chinese had a deep love of nature and a sincere belief that humankind is merely a subordinate constituent of nature. Even the emperor, who had absolute power, was merely the "son of heaven." The common interest of Chinese gardens was to recreate the image of nature while accommodating the sophisticated needs of imperial retreats or the ancient gentlemen scholars' resort houses within limited areas of various sizes. Therefore, more architecture is introduced into the space composition, incorporated with courtyards and partially concealed enclosures, all integrated as inseparable parts of the garden entity. From these basic ideas and needs derived the various principles that came to mold the style of the Chinese garden.

The traditional Chinese spatial presentation is characterized by the limitation of visibility to divisional sections designed to be exposed gradually. Sequential planning of space, pursuing a cumulative effect, is practiced both in the palaces, temples, and courtyard houses and in Chinese gardens, though the purposes are totally different (fig. 2.1). The spaces — whether in the form of enclosed, symmetrically laid out courts in the temples, palaces, and houses or artistically designed scenic sections in gardens — are invariably unfolded one by one in sequences that lead to a climax-fulfilling, individual purpose. The perfect order of the Imperial Palace in Beijing, very consistent with the absolutism of the ancient emperors, is rigidly imposed. The whole arrangement is one of extraordinary psychological force; the axial symmetrical planning and the enormous scale have been used to provide an expression of total power (fig. 3.1). The spatial climax is allocated to the emperor's and courtiers' audience hall, Taihe Dian, and its confronting court (5). The Temple of Heaven in Beijing, sequential space disposition with axial, symmetrical layout, is another example (fig. 3.2).

Spatial disposition in Chinese gardens is unlike that of a stately European edifice with landscaping approaches that enhance its magnificence and

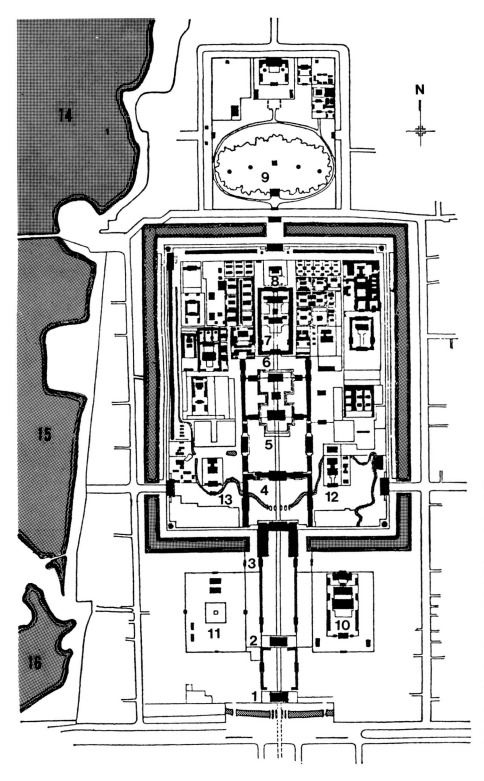

FIG. 3.1 *Master plan of the Imperial Palace, Beijing: (1) Tiann'an Men, Gate of Heavenly Peace; (2) Duan Men, Gate of Correctness; (3) Wu Men, Gate Meridian; (4) Taibe Men, Gate of Supreme Peace; (5) Taibe Dian, Hall of Supreme Peace; (6) Qianging Men, Gate of Universal Purity; (7) Qianging Gong, Hall of Universal Purity; (8) Yu Huayuan, Imperial Garden; (9) Jing Shan, Viewing Hill; (10) Tai Miao, Imperial Ancestral Temple; (11) Sheji Tan, Altar of God of Land and God of Grain; (12) Wenhua Dian, Literary Magnificence Hall; (13) Wuying Dian, Military Brilliance Hall; (14) Beihai, North Sea; (15) Zhonghai, Middle Sea; (16) Nanhai, South Sea.*

FIG. 3.2 *The Temple of Heaven, Beijing, with axial layout in sequential space disposition.*

achieve immediate visual effect. There is no point in a Chinese garden from which the entire garden scene is visible at a glance; this provides for a romantic adventure. Straight walks, long avenues, and well-balanced parterres resulted from the mathematical mind of the west. This aesthetic conception is fundamentally alien to Chinese taste. Ancient Chinese garden makers chose to avoid stiff orderliness and geometrical rigidity. Curves and studied irregularity generally characterize the design. In the Chinese garden, to make possible the myriads of vistas and various centers of interest, walkways are curved.

The land form is often undulating in contour so that vision is under control to provide changing views of varying sight ranges, and the climaxes organized in the scenic sections provide maximal visual satisfaction.

The acute contradiction between re-creating the vast space existing in wilderness and supplying the enormous amount of buildings demanded for human habitation had hampered Chinese garden design, but it had also generated the most wonderful and ingenious spatial disposition in the gardens. The vastness of space was simulated in limited, structured environments through deliberate ambiguity between "indoors" and "outdoors." The open space is treated as an extension of indoor living space; the buildings become the sheltered part of the garden entity (fig. 3.3). Thus, the concept of continuous space disposition was practiced in Chinese garden hundreds of years before the advent of continuous spatial design in the modern western world.

During the late 1950s, architectural design began to consider the concept of built environments. Design applied to environmental atmosphere has been part of western contemporary exploration. Frank Lloyd Wright's seemingly novel statement was:"Architecture is the scientific art of making structure express ideas." The Chinese garden, however, had long been built as an ideological environment. An air of profound tranquility is its basic pursuit. Every garden, and even its subdivided scenic sections, is endowed with inspirational quality by a specific emotional appeal.

Historical Affiliation

The first introduction of the Chinese garden to European countries can be traced back to Marco Polo's history of his travels to the Far East in the thirteenth century. All his praises of the landscape gardens were confirmed afterward by Jesuit French missionaries' letters from Beijing containing detailed descriptions of Chinese gardens. Landscape views painted on porcelain and wallpaper exported from China further introduced the enchanting landscape views of the Chinese garden. During the late seventeenth century—despite the maze and labyrinth invented in European gardens to satisfy the curious

FIG. 3.3 *Flowing space in the Chinese garden — the continuity of open space and interior space: O = open space; S = sheltered space defined from overhead; D = sheltered space further defined in plan by columns; I = interior space; C = courtyard space defined by walls but not sheltered.*

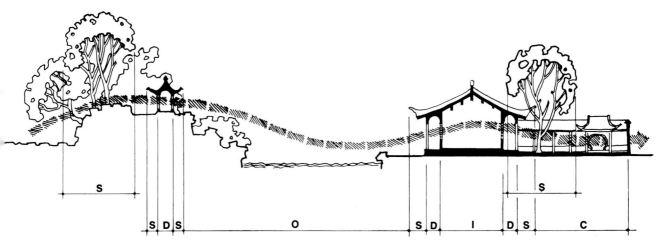

and to compensate for linear monotony—the English became bored with the open arrangement and far-reaching view of the classic garden. They began to favor the hills and creeks, groves and rocks of natural landscape.

The search began for a change in garden style. Admiration for natural landscape was expressed in the literature of that time; the charms of nature were captured in the landscapes of the French painters Nicolas Poussin, 1594–1665, and Claude Lorrain, 1600–1682, and the Italian painter Salvator Rosa, 1615–1673. The advent of a revolutionary garden style was inevitable.

The intimate integration of poetry, painting, and garden art led to the culmination of ancient Chinese garden art. An English poet, Alexander Pope, 1688–1744, also maintained that the garden should be built under the rules of painting. He began to experiment—integrating poetry, painting, and garden design in his own garden and the garden constructions of friends. His theory coincided precisely with that of Wang Wei, the Chinese poet and garden maker (699–759) of the Tang dynasty.

The pioneer of the English landscape garden, William Kent (1684–1748), deeply fascinated by landscape paintings of Nicolas Poussin and Salvator Rosa, was resolute in advocating garden building for the realization of ideal pictorial views on actual sites. His famous remark, "Nature abhors a straight line," corresponded with the Oriental garden tradition. Thomas Whateley was the first in the western world to suggest rocks as a garden component in his book *Observations on Modern Gardening,* written in 1770. The first application of rocks, recorded in ancient Chinese history, was found in Tu Yuan, the Rabbit Garden, built as early as the Western-Han dynasty (206–8 B.C.).

The English garden reached its culmination in the works of Lancelot Brown (1715–1783). In the late eighteenth century, a staff member of the West Indies Inc., William Chambers, visited many of the myriads of gardens then existing in Guangzhou. In 1761, he built the famous Kew Garden—in the London suburb—with a 10-story Chinese pagoda, a Confucius temple, and a China hall. His book *A Dissertation on Oriental Gardening,* published in 1772, highly praised the Chinese garden's artistic qualification.

Thus, Chinese garden art cross-fertilized with the West, influencing not only the English landscape gardens but also the modern gardens of all Europe. In France, the Chinese artificial hill was imitated in the sixteenth century and an experimental landscape garden had been built in 1700, much earlier than in England. The extent of the interest increased, however, after the transplanting of English landscape gardens to the Continent during the mid-eighteenth century. At the same time, letters from the French missionary P. Jean-Denis Attiret arrived in Paris with descriptions of Chinese gardens that aroused an enormous interest in them. The French acknowledged the close resemblance between the Chinese and English gardens and invented the term *Anglo-Chinois garden.* It was recorded that no less than twenty gardens with Chinese pavilion and bridges were built in Paris alone. Other French cities followed suit. Water pavilions, pagodas, and other Chinese garden features were as popular in Germany and were then transmitted to Hungary, Russia, and Sweden. The popularity of Chinese garden features in Europe continued till the 1830s.

FIG. 3.4 *The scenic West Lake in Hangzhou, Zhejiang Province.*

FIG. 3.5 *Fuxing Park, the former French Park, Shanghai, with geometric parterres.*

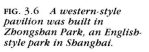

FIG. 3.6 *A western-style pavilion was built in Zhongshan Park, an English-style park in Shanghai.*

The English and the French first opened large tracts of land for public use as parks in the eighteenth century. The accommodation of scenic spots for public interest in China had a much longer history. During the Song dynasty (960–1279), more than ten famous gardens in the ancient capital city Bianliang were listed for public tours in springtime. Gardens of that period were also built as attractions in restaurants and temples. The scenic West Lake in Hangzhou, Zhejiang Province, for example, was used for spring outings in the South-Song dynasty (1127–1279) (fig. 3.4). Hangzhou was then the capital city, called Lin'an. Even the imperial gardens were opened to the public each spring for more than a month.

As for western garden influence over China, the most significant was the French-style garden with architecture of strong European baroque flavor, introduced by a French missionary, the Jesuit Father Benoit, in Yuanming Yuan, Beijing (plan 16). Different types of European classic architecture and parks were built in the former colonial concessions of the larger Chinese cities. A good example is the French Park, Fuxing Park at present, in Shanghai's former French colonial concession. Its main garden feature is typical geometrical parterres (fig. 3.5). Another example is an English landscape garden, Zhongshan Park at present, in the former English concession (fig. 3.6). The English landscape parks, with undulating naturalistic land forms and extensive grass lawns, have a scale that better accommodates the needs of the visiting multitudes. These English landscape parks had considerable influence over modern China's public parks and private house gardens. The geometrical French garden style scarcely attracted any real interest in China.

During the last decade, public parks have boomed in Chinese cities, old and new. Recreational parks are being built in smaller, rural towns as well. A pleasing effort is being made to create an innovative modern Chinese garden style—with the fascinations of the traditional Chinese garden art—while at the same time coping adequately with the needs of the enormous Chinese population.

CHAPTER FOUR

Comparison of the Chinese and Japanese Garden

When compared to the geometric and architectonic gardens of the European tradition, the Chinese and the Japanese gardens are alike in projecting a natural appearance. With other aspects of their culture, the Japanese learned about garden design from the Chinese — first through Koreans and later by means of direct intercourse with China. Early in 552, Buddhism was introduced to Japan from China through Korea. During the Sui dynasty of China, in the twentieth year of Empress Suiko's reign in Japan, in the year A.D. 613, Soma Wakako learned Chinese garden art from Korea and constructed the first garden in Japan. The Japanese garden initially adopted the Chinese model of Qin and Han dynasty style with the construction of "Immortal Islands in the Sea." Thus began the typical thematic scenery of famous Japanese gardens, such as those in the temple Saiho-ji in Kyoto and the upper garden in Shuga-kuin Detached Palace. Later in the Song dynasty, the Japanese came under the Chinese influence of Zen Buddhism and the appreciation of tea. Meanwhile, the foundation was laid for the full bloom of Japanese garden art.

A courtier of the overthrown Ming dynasty, Zhu Shunshui, exiled himself to Japan and introduced the "gardens of the literati" through his lectures. Chinese landscape paintings of the Song and Ming dynasties were copied into

FIG. 4.1 *Sand garden in the Japanese Tea Garden, San Francisco.*

Japanese water-and-ink paintings and compiled as garden-building references.

Japanese gardens, garden architecture, and garden scenes are mostly entitled and inscribed with artistic Chinese calligraphy as an expression of classical grace. All of them clearly demonstrate the profound influence of Chinese garden art in Japan, which caused the resemblance of these two schools of oriental garden art. As a result of its maturation — during the Ashikaga (1336–1572) and Tokugawa (1603–1867) periods — Japanese garden art finally outgrew the Chinese influence. Characterized by simplicity and symbolic expression, endowed with a strong tendency toward abstraction, the Japanese garden had evolved into a unique style of its own, a style that acquired worldwide influence.

There are, however, major differences between the Chinese and Japanese gardens, and these differences deserve our special attention. In terms of general layout, the Chinese garden stresses mobile viewing, while more of the earlier Japanese gardens were designed for static viewing and paths were totally absent. The observer was expected to be content with inaccessible three-dimensional picture gardens, meant to be viewed from the *engawas,* verandas, of the buildings. Therefore, garden scenes could be greatly reduced in scale to cope with the scarcity of space in mountainous Japan.

Paths are found, however, in Japanese "strolling gardens," built in later periods, designed specifically for viewing when walking from one important scenic point to another, and in the "tea gardens," created to meet the needs of special rituals connected with the tea ceremony. In the Chinese garden, the touring route — for mobile viewing — is virtually an indispensable part of the garden.

Naturalistic landscape scenes in both gardens are reduced in scale, but the actual dimensions are usually more generous in Chinese gardens to allow participation in the simulated natural environment.

Perfection of composition seems to be consciously sought after in Japanese gardens. At least, the effect of those exquisitely designed garden scenes lends visitors a feeling of being self-conscious lest their personal intrusion violate the precise balance of composition. In one type of meditation garden, sand or pebbles are raked or contoured to represent the idealized flow of water (fig. 4.1). Even plants can be taboo in extreme examples of the Japanese "dry landscape" garden. One interpretation would be that the elimination of all living elements contributes to the absolute control required for the creation of "perfect beauty."

The Chinese garden, however, allows imperfection and expects the garden to be inspired by the beauty of natural growth. Even the windblown algae collected at the edge of a pond can be appreciated as part of the natural beauty.

The most obvious difference between these two oriental gardens is the variation in style and arrangement of the architectural elements. The architecture in Japanese gardens is relatively independent, though complete harmony between garden and building is the aim. Usually, gardens provide views for buildings. In another arrangement, temple gardens are connected with the surrounding landscape to serve as a foil for buildings.

In the Chinese solution — since architecture is an inextricable and thoroughly integrated component of the garden view — gardens are more densely constructed, with different types of buildings throughout the composition or at least in the garden's major portion.

Most of the existing gardens in China are built or remodeled in the elaborate and decorative late Ming or Qing dynasty style. Rustic forms from periods prior to the early Ming dynasty had often been depicted in ancient Chinese landscape paintings, and praised in the traditional poetry of earlier times. Such elements as thatched-roof gates and bamboo or wooden terraces and fences were part of a "purified" life that defied worldly vanity. Unfortunately, these elements can only be found in Japanese gardens today.

Certain architectural features, smaller in size and simpler in form — such as stone basins for collecting spring water, stone lanterns, and wells — are typical features in Japan and, to an extent, characterize their gardens. Many of these elements, once favored in ancient China, had been discarded in most later Chinese gardens. Recently, during the restoration in a Shanghai suburb of a Ming dynasty garden, Guyi Yuan, the Ancient Magnificent Garden, an ancient stone lantern and stone pillars, *chuang,* were adopted from historical ruins. These relics were used to enrich the cultural interest of the garden

FIG. 4.2 *A stone lantern in Guyi Yuan, the Ancient Magnificent Garden, Shanghai.*

FIG. 4.3 *Jianzheng Memorial Hall in Yangzhou, Jiangsu Province.*

according to Chinese tradition; being absent from existing, more famous gardens, however, the occasional appearance of ancient features seems exotic to the Chinese (fig. 4.2).

A Buddhist temple, the Toshodaiji, was built in Nara (ancient Heijo), Japan, by a Chinese monk, Jianzheng (Ganjin to the Japanese). He arrived in the archipelago in A.D. 753 with the transmission of Buddhism as his principal mission. A highly cultivated scholar, he had brought with him the arts of painting, sculpture, calligraphy, and architecture, together with other forms of Tang dynasty Chinese culture. In 1963, a reproduction of this temple was erected in China, in the city of Yangzhou, Jiangsu Province (fig. 4.3). This temple was built to accommodate the special reception for the gilded image of Jianzheng, brought from Japan for a visit to his motherland. This temporary display of Jian Zheng's statue in China was held in the year of 1963 to commemorate the 1200th anniversary of his death. It was a gesture of friendship between the Chinese and Japanese peoples. Interestingly enough, this temple of Tang dynasty style was mistaken for Japanese architecture by many Chinese. It seems that the Japanese traditional architecture retains a reasonably pure form of the Tang dynasty, while the Chinese have become more familiar with the elaborate architectural style of late Ming and Qing dynasties.

Rocks are loved by both the Chinese and the Japanese, but they are manipulated in quite different ways. The most distinctive difference relates to the quantity of stone used. Fewer rocks are applied in Japanese garden compositions and they are treated with a more succinct manner. Rocks smaller in size and simpler in form, compared to those of the Chinese gardens, are presented individually, scattered on the ground in vertical, horizontal, or half-buried forms, in elegant compositions involving various dispositions and intervening distances.

Many celebrated Chinese gardens, on the other hand, boast a collection of magnificent, huge, monolithic rocks or an extraordinary quantity of rockeries piled up to reproduce a traversable, constructed, three-dimensional wilderness of enormous size.

Certain differences can be observed in the way plant material is utilized. The Japanese garden is distinguished by plants trimmed into geometrical forms (fig. 4.1). Plants are pruned into artistic forms for individual appreciation. Plants in Chinese gardens are more often presented in group compositions, which allows their appearance to manifest the beauty of natural growth, and plants with geometrical forms do not suit the Chinese taste.

The refined elegance of Chinese private gardens is ascribed to the aesthetic inherent in the traditional water-and-ink painting. Monochromatic paintings, with their inexhaustible gradations, are deemed as interesting and perhaps more enchanting than color paintings. Peonies and camellias are loved for their gorgeous blossoms, but they are dominated by green leaves when seen at a distance and therefore harmonize well with the garden entity. Colorful flowers are preferred for close-up observation and are more often used for indoor or courtyard display. There, they are cultivated in flower beds or portable pots of various size. The azalea in full bloom, with its massive and imposing colors, could be taken as the boldest touch in Chinese gardens, where it is often dispersed on rockeries and artificial hills. The blossoming of the plum, cherry, and peach groves is favored in both the Chinese and Japanese gardens for its dainty color and seasonal expression.

Japanese gardens require enormous work and the skill of talented gardeners with artistic taste in pruning to maintain the visual balance of growing plants. They employ more plants as important garden features for individual appreciation, so replanting is inevitable to retain compositional balance.

The traditional Chinese garden, differing from the Japanese garden, can be seen as a balanced ecosystem. Its components have been selectively chosen and strategically placed in the garden, the result of experimentation by trial and error throughout the garden-building history of China. The choice of materials, from a wide variety of indigenous natural resources, has been passed down from generation to generation as part of garden art. The Chinese garden—with its hills, water, plants, fish, fowl, and architecture—is an artificial environment modeled after natural ones.

The cycling of resources operates in a mutually compatible manner. For example, water fowl—such as mandarin ducks—feed on the fish; they, in turn, fertilize the plants, such as lotus and water chestnuts. Goldfish feed on the water weeds and limit their growth. The artificial pond is often a pool of stagnant water, but it is far from being a body of dead matter. Even the architecture of the garden contributes as wind shields and sun shelters for delicate, shade-loving plants. On the other hand, Chinese garden architecture, with its open style, affords adequate solar and wind control to benefit the growth of plants. There is not much need for periodic replanting, pruning, replenishing of fish stock, and feeding the fowl; little maintenance is required. In this way, a delicate balance is maintained once a Chinese garden has been established. Thus, the unique merit of the Chinese garden is based on the self-sustaining natural balance that is ultimately achieved. It is not merely a replica of nature; it *is* nature!

CHAPTER FIVE

Classification of Chinese Gardens

The classic gardens of China include the private garden, the imperial garden, and the temple garden, among which Buddhist or Taoist temples are the best models of nature reformed into constructed environments that integrate the beauty of natural landscape with artifacts. The most fascinating scenic spots in China's mountainous regions were chosen for the construction of Buddhist or Taoist monasteries and temples (fig. 5.1). It was well remarked that "No mountain was ever devoid of monks." A serene and peaceful atmosphere was sought to assist the monks and priests in removing themselves from mortal concerns and becoming closer to the heavenly "paradise." Constructions were erected to accommodate the religious requirements and the daily needs of the monks and priests. The peculiarities or inspiration of the sites tremendously evoked the imaginations of the ingenious monks. Buildings highlight the mountainscape and, in the meantime, provide a command of landscape views in the vicinity. As lovers of nature, the monks not only discovered but also reorganized and, with their artistic taste, intensified the beauty of the landscape.

   The mundane world learned of these gardens through religious pilgrimages. Only a few of the numerous examples are the scenic mountains Huang Shan, Tianyun Shan, and Jiuhua Shan in Anhui Province; Tai Shan in Shandong Province; Hua Shan in Shanxi Province; Emei Shan in Sichuan Province; and Tianmu Shan in Zhejiang Province. Architectural complexes were planned and built with courtyards and gardens intermingling so intimately with their natural environment that the modern "organic architecture" of the western world could be traced back more than 2000 years in China.

Nevertheless, the layout of the temples can be traced to the tenets of traditional landscape painting. The temples, in their turn, were constantly depicted in the celebrated antique landscape paintings. Temple gardens, as gardens, however, are often designed as constituents of the temple or monastery building complex. These cultivated gardens are generally simpler in composition, mostly in the form of courtyard gardens. Therefore, Chinese traditional gardens are generally classified into two major types — the private gardens of the south and the imperial gardens of the north — and the temple gardens are not included.

Gardens in different regions maintain distinctive characteristics due to the occupants' functional needs and aesthetic interests, regional artistic expressions of different historical periods, and the availability of plants, building material, and techniques.

Private Gardens of South China (fig. 5.2)

The south gardens can be further classified into the gardens south of the river Chang Jiang and the gardens in south China. The traditional gardens in south China, mostly located south of the mountain Nan Ling in the provinces of Guangdong and Guangxi, are now being explored, restored, and extended to function as public parks. According to the present explorations, the gardens tend to be small in size, ebullient and piquant in character. They are famous for their open-space disposition, made possible by the warm climate that nurtures an ample variety of tropical plants.

Gardens south of the river Chang Jiang are mostly located in the river's southern delta, in the provinces of Jiangsu and Zhejiang. The lower reach of Chang Jiang is called the Yangzi River. The residential private gardens in this region are graceful and refined and close to the subtle harmony of the wilderness, with modesty and simplicity fostering a tone of restrained elegance. Suzhou, Yangzhou, Wuxi, and Nanjing in Jiangsu Province and Hangzhou in Zhejiang Province are the cities in the Yangzi River's southern delta to which the garden builders flocked.

Suzhou, famed as the "city of gardens," is endowed with over a hundred high-quality surviving gardens. The Suzhou gardens are celebrated not only as being the most beautiful and distinctive but also as representing most clearly the ideas of Chinese garden design. Therefore, more examples from the Suzhou gardens will be discussed later in this book to illustrate the basic garden design principles. The earliest Suzhou gardens, still in existence, date back to the tenth century, in the late Tang dynasty: the garden Canglang Ting, the Gentle Wave Pavilion, and Huanxiu Shanzhuang, the Grace-Surrounding Mountain Villa. Generally, the longer a garden's history, the less it retains its original design, because of repeated alterations by successive owners. Most

FIG. 5.1 *Tiantong Si, a temple in Ningbo, Zhejiang Province.*

FIG. 5.2 *Shizi Lin, the Lion Grove, Suzhou.*

FIG. 5.3 *The Spring View, composed of bamboo and stone bamboo shoots, in Ge Yuan, the Isolated Garden or the Garden of Bamboo Leaves, Yangzhou, Jiangsu Province.*

Suzhou gardens existing today were first built or reconstructed in the Qing dynasty, in the last half of the nineteenth century.

Suzhou's mild weather and plentiful water are favorable to horticulture. These are not only ideal conditions for garden making, but they promoted the agricultural productivity that contributed to a thriving economy in the area. Road and canal systems connected with the Grand Canal—which is one of ancient China's great feats, running north-south across the country—and further facilitated communication and laid a foundation for the city of Suzhou as a center of cultural activities and superior crafts, such as fine brickwork and carpentry. These benefits induced the upper classes to flock to Suzhou for residence. It satisfied their needs and desire for amusement and provided cultural satisfaction to their artist friends. Thus, poets, painters, and artisan masters pooled their talents for design, construction, and cultivation. The Suzhou gardens flourished, presenting all the wonderful characteristics of Chinese garden art.

The more celebrated gardens in Suzhou are: Zhouzheng Yuan, the Unsuccessful Politician's Garden, also translated as the Humble Administrator's Garden (plan 1); Wangshi Yuan, the Net Master's Garden, also translated as the Fisherman's Garden (plan 2); Liu Yuan, the Lingering Garden (plan 3); Shizi Lin, the Lion Grove (plan 4); Canglang Ting, the Surging-Wave Pavilion (plan 5); Yi Yuan, the Pleasure Garden (plan 6); and Huanxiu Shanzhuang, the Grace-Surrounding Mountain Villa (plan 7).

Under similar conditions, gardens proliferated in Yangzhou and other cities. The ancient city of Yangzhou, prospering as a trading center connecting northern China to the south through the Grand Canal, had greatly attracted merchants for residence. Thus, Yangzhou became second in quantity of gardens and boasts a unique integration of the south and north garden styles.

FIG. 5.4 *Beihai Gongyuan, the North Sea Park, Beijing.*

Due to social and historical background, gardens in Yangzhou are apt to display the owners' wealth rather than the cultivated grace typical of the Suzhou gardens.

Jixiao Shanzhuang, the Roar-Resounding Mountain Villa (plan 9) and Ge Yuan are the two of the best gardens in Yangzhou well restored to their original elegance. Ge Yuan (plan 8) means the Bamboo Leaves Garden or the Isolated Garden. The name was chosen to indicate that the garden was dominated by bamboo, because the Chinese word *ge* resembles a cluster of bamboo leaves in typical traditional Chinese painting (fig. 5.3). This is a good example of the enchanting Chinese naming art. (The literal translation is the Isolated Garden.)

Jichang Yuan, Carefree-Abiding Garden, in Wuxi (plan10), Zhan Yuan, the Looking-Forward Garden, in Nanjing (plan 11), and Yu Yuan, the Pleasing Garden, in Shanghai (plan 12) are all reconstructed to manifest Chinese garden art through the efforts of present-day architects. Numerous gardens in cities and towns throughout China, especially in this region, are being explored, restored to their original magnificence, and extended to accommodate modern needs.

Imperial Gardens of North China (fig. 5.4)

Beijing, the ancient capital of Yuan, Ming, and Qing dynasties, was the center of garden building in north China. The predominance of its imperial gardens was chiefly accomplished during the reign of the last dynasty, Qing. Imperial gardens of the north tend toward staidness and resplendence consistent with

FIG. 5.5 *The rubble stone enclosure wall of Bishu Shangzhuang, the Summer-Retreating Mountain Villa, Chengde, Hebei Province, undulates with the contour.*

a sense of palatial grandeur. Special approaches are employed in dealing with form, coloring, and the sense of beauty. Roofs of yellow-glazed tiles are set off by green foliage, blue sky, and an extensive span of water surfaces. Multicolored beams and brackets under the embellished eaves are supported by rows of brilliant vermilion pillars.

Many of the imperial garden scenes are reproductions of distinguished gardens throughout the country, especially the scenic landscape interests and gardens south of the Yangzi River. Emperor Qianlong of the Qing dynasty, after his legendary visits to southern China, demanded that the greatest landscape views and garden scenes be reproduced and included in his gardens. He ordered his court painters to record the garden scenes he chose for reference in constructing his own gardens. Direct imitation by the north imperial gardens of scenic spots and private gardens in the south then began. Typical examples are found in the thirty-six scenes of Bishu Shanzhuang, the Summer-Retreating Mountain Villa, in Chengde, Hebei Province, and the twenty-four scenes of Yihe Yuan, the Summer Palace in Beijing. These scenes are microcosms of the riches of the vast empire's celebrated gardens and landscape views.

The Summer-Retreating Mountain Villa is located 250 kilometers northeast of Beijing. It covers an area of 8400 *mu* (1 *mu* equals 667 square meters) and is enclosed by a rubble stone wall measuring 20 *li* (fig. 5.5). (A single Chinese *li* equals 500 meters.) There were seventy-two garden scenes originally built in this retreating palace; each scene was given a poetic name. (The tradition of entitling scenic views started from the celebrated Ten Scenes of the West Lake in the city of Hangzhou.) Some scenes in the Summer-Retreating Mountain Villa had explanatory names that referred to the particular scene's original model. The Surging-Wave Isle, for example, is an inner garden imitating a Suzhou garden, Surging-Wave Pavilion; the Mist and Rain Mansion (fig. 5.6) reproduces the Mist and Rain Mansion in Jiaxing (fig. 5.7), Zhejiang Province;

FIG. 5.6 *Yanyu Lou, Mist and Rain Mansion, in Bishu Shanizhuang, the Summer-Retreating Mountain Villa, Chengde, Hebei Province.*

FIG. 5.7 *Yanyu Lou, Mist and Rain Mansion, Jiaxing, Zhejiang Province.*

FIG. 5.8 *Xiao Jin Shan, the Little Golden Hill, in the Summer-Retreating Mountain Villa, Chengde, Hebei Province.*

FIG. 5.9 *Jinshan Si, the Golden Hill Temple, Zhenjiang, Jiangsu Province.*

FIG. 5.10 *Longevity Hill and the lake, Kunming Hu, in the Summer Palace, Beijing*

FIG. 5.11 *A long walking gallery stretching along a pond and connected to a pavilion in the Summer-Retreating Mountain Villa, Chengde, Heibei Province.*

the Little Golden Hill (fig. 5.8) imitates the Golden Hill of Zhenjiang (fig. 5.9), Jiangsu Province; and the Lion Grove Cultural Garden took the garden Lion Grove in Suzhou as its model.

Kunming Lake in the Summer Palace (plan 14.A), including the picturesque causeways, covers a vast area of 200 hectares, which is nearly three-fourths of the garden's total area. It was completely constructed, to reproduce scenic West lake in Hangzhou, on the orders of Emperor Qianlong. The stately Longevity Hill (fig. 5.10) was built from the earth excavated to form Kunming Lake. A Suzhou street replica was even created along the back lake of the Summer Palace so that the imperial family could enjoy bargaining as ordinary people in fascinating small shops, with eunuchs disguised as shop-keepers to fulfill their pleasure.

In the Imperial Palace—formerly called the Forbidden City and now the Palace Museum—three large lakes, including the famed lake, Beihai, the North Sea, were all artificially created. The construction started in 1179, during the Jin dynasty (1115–1234), continued through Ming dynasty, and was completed in Qing dynasty.

Xiequ Yuan, the Garden of Harmonious Interest (plan 14-D), in the north-eastern corner of the Summer Palace, is an imitation of the Jichang Garden in Wuxi (plan 10.A). This "garden within a garden" is small and elegant, with pavilions and walking galleries winding around a placid pond. It successfully reproduced the beauty of its model.

The famed scenic spots and the successful southern private gardens inspired the artistic creativity of the imperial gardens of Qing dynasty that were built in northern China. Nevertheless, these reproductions were not simply copies of the originals but had been revised according to the peculiarities of their site. Therefore, the north imperial gardens remained innovative by retaining the garden-designing canon: "Follow the environmental context and manifest the best." They were also embellished with imperial splendor and architecture of the northern style.

In order to cope with the site dimensions, and the grandeur and extravagance demanded by imperial customs, the imperial garden architecture and other garden features have little or no reduction in scale, unlike the private gardens. Drastic differences in size and elegance between the private and imperial gardens can be taken as one important reason for the diversified design of scenic features. Crooked and curvilinear pathways prevail in private gardens as a means of creating seeming spaciousness in small areas. As for the imperial gardens—such as the Beihai Park and the Summer Palace—they occupy thousands of *mu* and are built on such a large scale that there is apparently no scarcity of land. On the contrary, effective measures were needed to facilitate communication among different parts of the vast plots. Therefore, straight passages, generally absent from Chinese private gardens, are used for fast access. Walking galleries of enormous length were erected in the Summer Palace, the Beihai Park, and the Summer-Retreating Mountain Villa in Chengde (fig. 5.11) and they became specialties of these gardens.

The axial layout, generally excluded from Chinese private gardens, seems indispensable to imperial needs and expression. In the Summer Palace, the entrance is strictly symmetrical. Another axis is set at the center of the Kunming Lake's shore (plan 14.A), starting with a gorgeous three-bay arch, *bailuo,* and rising to the top of Longevity Hill with an ensemble of buildings and courts dominated by an octagonal tower, the Hall of Buddha Fragrance. Due to the vastness of the area covered, the axial layout is well blended into the naturalistic garden by means of numerous architectural complexes planned in more vivid informal design with garden features as transitions. The ancient Chinese garden makers were careful in dealing with varying contexts, following a canon of garden design: "To be guided but not bounded by principles."

Another striking difference between imperial and private gardens is the use of color. The architecture in the private gardens, including those in the northern cities, tends to be elegant and subtle in form and subdued in color. The characteristic color scheme of whitewashed wall, blue-black tiled roof, and woodwork painted in chestnut brown is only occasionally enlivened by color of mild intensity. This, enhanced by the reflection of a placid pond, unfailingly fosters an atmosphere of extraordinary serenity (fig. 1.5). In the enormous imperial gardens of northern China, which has relatively less sunshine all year round, the buildings are accented with brilliant colors, which put the focus on scenes that might otherwise be lost in the vast range of garden views. Likewise, the celebrated artworks, such as paintings, are often heightened by strokes of bold colors.

These distinctive variations between imperial and private gardens can be explained by the differing aesthetic criteria and emotional expression. The imperial gardens strove for grandeur and splendid luxury, while the private gardens possess modesty and poetic grace.

PART TWO

Components

*The formation of hills and water took priority in the process of
structuring the naturalistic landscape garden. Architecture,
attempting to provide living space as well as scenic features,
dominates the Chinese garden in an extraordinary way.
Plants are naturally indispensable. Literature and art are
incorporated in an exceptional way, contributing to Chinese
garden art's unique ability to supply cultural satisfaction. All
these constitute the essential components of the Chinese garden.*

CHAPTER SIX

Hills and Water

The shape of the land is the foundation of the landscape and the basis of all gardens, oriental or occidental. Chinese landscape painting is called *shan-shui hua,* which means the painting of mountains and water. This clearly indicates that mountain and water are taken as dominating elements and are the most appreciated subjects in landscape scenes. Old Chinese literature asserted that water constitutes the "arteries" of the garden, while the hills represent its "skeleton" and the plants are merely the "hair." "Digging ponds and piling hills" was a common Chinese term for garden making.

Hill Molding (fig. 6.1)

The artificial hill is the Chinese garden's most unconventional and fascinating garden feature, indispensable to its unique style. "Hill molding and rockery manipulation" was a term in ancient China for garden construction. Artificial hills are the essential scenic features and also function as space-confining structural components. Rock manipulation generally serves to enrich the vertical composition of a confined space within the garden (fig. 6.2).

The artificial hill is molded to simulate the distilled and enhanced beauty of natural mountain views—peak, cliff, precipice, ravine, gorge, and cave. The forms of cordillera lend vivid expressions of majestic, perilous, or esoteric effects according to the garden maker's artistic interpretation. An artificial hill's sculptural composition is based on the availability of rock for the project and the physical characteristics of the rock to be used.

Artificial hills were molded by specialized artisans, respected as master craftsmen, possessing sophisticated artistic tastes. Ji Cheng, the author of

Yuan Ye, was one of China's most famous rockery masters in addition to being a great painter and garden maker.

Hill molding can be traced back to a remote time before the written history of China. This early type of artificial hill was constructed with the soil excavated from digging the watercourse. Balancing the soil on site saved the labor of conveyance. This economic reason greatly fostered "hills and water" compositions as an essential theme and soil balancing became a preliminary step to building Chinese gardens. Hills are often asymmetric in shape, with a steeper slope on one end — depicting a precipitous cliff — that contrasts with a moderate slope on the other side. Their artistic silhouette also results from a rational construction process whereby manual labor piled and conveyed the soil; the inclined slope facilitated this process. Technically, since the soil required reclining angles to form stabilized hills, it was impossible to construct tall, upright forms — such as peaks, cliffs, gorges, ravines, or other mountain features — without the support of rocks as retaining elements. Due

FIG. 6.1 *The Grand Artificial Hill in Yu Yuan, the Pleasing Garden, Shanghai, is famous as the largest and best example of an artificial hill, made of yellow stone. The River View Pavilion, built on the artificial hill, was dedicated to viewing the river scene of Huang-pu Jiang in olden times, when there were no obstructing taller buildings.*

to weathering, the outline of a soil hill might result in an uninteresting and plain appearance.

Rocks were also indispensable as decorative details in completing the artificial hill. Thus, the composite use of soil and rocks was not only critical to the formation and style of the artificial hill but immensely affected the consumption of material and labor, and the cost of garden construction.

There are three methods of hill molding in regard to the use of soil and rocks: The first type, the earth hill, is suitable for gardens with large tracts of land, such as those of the palatial gardens. The hill on the Jade Flower Isle was constructed with the soil extracted to form the lake, Beihai (plan 15). The hill was large enough to be cultivated extensively with plants that made it seem like a natural mountain (fig. 5.4). Trees added height to such hills and fostered a majestic look. This approach, however, is not suitable for constructing smaller hills. Tall trees planted on a small hill result in a dwarfing effect, causing the hill to look lower in comparison to the height of the trees.

A naturally stabilized soil hill required a proportionately large base to secure its height. A clumsy bermlike look resulted when a small-scale hill was built solely with soil. Since qualities of loftiness and gracefulness were sought in reproducing the natural landscape, hills entirely built with soil had limited use in Chinese gardens.

The second type of artificial hill construction is the composite use of soil and rocks. This method can be classified in two different ways. Building a hill mainly with soil, complemented with rocks, was an effective and practical way of molding larger artificial hills. The hills in the Lingering Garden and the Surging-Wave Pavilion garden in Suzhou are earth hills surrounded at the foot with rocks about 3 feet high for retaining purposes as well as ornamentation (fig. 6.3). The crooked paths winding up the hills are lined with rocks for the same reasons (fig. 6.4). Rocks were often partially buried in the ground to give an illusion that the natural rock base of the land had been exposed by weathering.

Another method of molding soil and rock hills is to construct the hills mainly with rocks, supplemented with soil. In this method, there is a gigantic rockery constructed either with a solid soil base covered with rocks (fig. 6.5) or as a hollow structure built with rocks that can be shaped into mysterious caves and grottos enclosed within the artificial hills (fig. 6.6). The crevices and hollows of large-scale rockeries were often partially covered or filled with soil for plantings (fig. 6.7). Plants of limited growth were preferred in these areas, and vines and ferns were favored for a natural and appealing appearance. Additional soil was sometimes applied to the less obvious parts of a hill.

FIG. 6.2 (opposite, top left) *A rockery display with whitewashed wall as the backdrop at the entry of Wangshi Yuan, the Net Master's Garden, Suzhou.*

FIG. 6.3 (opposite, bottom) *An earth hill with rocks at the foot for retaining purposes as well as ornamentation; in Jichang Yuan, the Carefree-Abiding Garden, Wuxi.*

FIG. 6.4 (opposite, top right) *A crooked path winding up the hill is lined with rocks, a most decorative retaining device. Stairs built of rocks, leading to an elevated or multistoried building, are a favorite garden feature.*

FIG. 6.5 (top left) *The artificial hill in Xi Yuan, the West Garden, in Yangzhou.*

FIG. 6.6 (top right) *A crooked bridge leads to the cave in an artificial hill, built of lake rock, in Shizi Lin, the Lion Grove, Suzhou.*

FIG. 6.7 *A rockery arch spanning the watercourse, in Zhuozheng Yuan, the Unsuccessful Politician's Garden, Suzhou, adds greatly to the depth and serenity of the water scene. Vines and plants drooping on the rockery further introduce a natural look.*

The rear of the dominating hill in Suzhou's Unsuccessful Politician's Garden is mainly constructed with soil. This method cuts down on costly rock consumption. It also allows trees to be planted on the back of the slope, making the hill appear loftier and more natural.

The third type of artificial hill molding, the rock hills, is best applied in smaller constructions and in confined area. An ancient Chinese artist, Li Liweng, asserted in his *Li-weng's Random Collections:* "Rockery on a small scale is easy to handle; the larger the rockery, the harder the project is to accomplish." He also maintained: "The art of artificial hill presentation should stress the expression of a particular spirit rather than the pursuit of its physical dimensions." The sizable rock hill constructions that came into vogue during the Ming and Qing dynasties were not only expensive and labor consuming to build but also required highly qualified craftsmen to direct the projects. There are some gaudy examples—unsuccessful, costly arrays of rocks—that fail as pieces of art.

Artificial hills, both molded hills and rockery, were essential structural garden components in dividing space, screening, and serving as foils for garden views. Elegant sets of artificial hills were often built as ornamental screens at garden gates. Artificial hills were also employed to half screen an overpowering whitewashed plastered wall that, in its turn, served as a foil to the hill composition—promoting an artistic silhouette of the hills or rockeries (fig. 6.2). The rockeries were sometimes used as favorable partitions between scenic sections and were very effective transitions between artifacts and the natural garden landscape (figs. 6.8, 6.9). Artificial hills, when applied as the central scene of a garden, often served as elevated vantage points commanding panoramas of sectional garden scenes or landscapes of the vicinity. When the scale of the hills allows, a pavilion is appreciated as a viewing station and greatly highlights the "mountain view" (fig. 6.1). In crowning the hill with a pavilion or some other sizable feature, it is best to place the object off center from the tip of the peak, at a declining point for better aesthetic satisfaction (fig. 6.10). When organized appropriately in relation to other garden features, the artificial hill is always the most appreciated art presentation of the Chinese garden.

Manipulation of Rocks

There are basically two methods of rock application in the Chinese garden: One is to use rocks in constructing artificial hills, as mentioned previously, and the other is in the form of a rockery display known as the "manipulation of rocks." Rockery can be presented singly as a sculpture, ranging in size from a small desk decoration (fig. 6.11) up to a tall monolith (fig. 6.2). Rockery can also be composed into group compositions using the stones of the same type that differ in height or shape and are piled or positioned in multifarious ways. Rocks are used to decorate the embankments of watercourses (fig. 6.12) and to denote turning or transitional points of the garden scenes (figs. 6.13, 6.14); they are extensively applied to construct flower beds (figs. 2.5, 6.2), steps, and open-air stairs (fig. 6.4). These are the more effective and less expensive rockery presentations.

Artistic quality is achieved only when visual balance exists in all directions. The rockery presentation can best be fully manifested through unlimited imagination provoked by an appreciation of the magnificent artistic shapes observed in nature.

In the Lion Grove garden, exquisite and dainty lake rocks were sculptured to depict the lively actions of lions of all ages and sizes (fig. 6.15). Despite the amusing resemblance of the rock-sculptured lions to real ones, this type of realistic rockery manipulation is not considered by connoisseurs as an admirable, subtle piece of artwork because its images are limited to realistic objects, the lions. Rockery presentations are expected to evoke personal feelings through abstract beauty that inspires the unlimited enjoyment of reminiscence and thus allows for different interpretations, varying with moods or perspectives, as do the changing clouds in the sky. This conception of rockery art, characteristic of the Chinese garden maker, is unique.

As China is a country with a fantastic natural landscape of unimaginable variety, so the Stone Forest in Yunnan Province is one of China's major natural spectacles with its fascinating rocky cliffs that strikingly resemble human and animal postures. These dramatic mountain features have fanciful descriptive names given them by the local people and former tourists to provoke the interest and imagination of visitors who followed. The Stone Forest is enthusiastically accepted as a great natural attraction by tourists from all over the world. The rockery scenes of the Lion Grove garden, on the other hand,

FIG. 6.8 (top left) *Rocks are used as a transitional feature, dispersed around a pavilion built upon a pond, in Zhuozheng Yuan, the Unsuccessful Politician's Garden, Suzhou.*

FIG. 6.9 (bottom right) *A wall in Bishu Shanzhuang, the Summer-Retreating Mountain Villa, Chengde, is adorned with rockeries as the transition to the lake.*

FIG. 6.10 (top right) *Jinshan Si, the Golden Hill Temple, Zhenjiang, Jiangsu Province. A spectacular tower built at a declining point forms an exquisite silhouette.*

FIG. 6.11 (top left) *A small rockery is displayed in a hall in the garden Shizi Lin, the Lion Grove, Suzhou.*

FIG. 6.12 (top right) *Yellow rocks are used for building the embankment in Zhuozheng Yuan, the Unsuccessful Politician's Garden, Suzhou.*

FIG. 6.13 (bottom left) *Piled rockeries are displayed at the turning of two-story walking galleries in the Sound-Resounding Mountain Villa, Yangzhou. They greatly modify the overpowering effect of an excessive number of buildings in the garden.*

FIG. 6.14 (bottom right) *A bridge in Guyi Yuan, the Ancient Magnificent Garden, Shanghai, is accented by rocks at each end.*

FIG. 6.15 (top)   *In the garden Shizi Lin, the Lion Grove, Suzhou, gigantic rockeries were sculptured to resemble groups of lions of varied ages, in diversified activities.*

FIG. 6.16 (bottom left)   *The Crest-Cloud Peak in Liu Yuan, the Lingering Garden, Suzhou.*

FIG. 6.17 (bottom right)   *A piled rockery presentation with concealed joints; in the Slender West Lake, Yangzhou.*

should be taken as an enrichment of Chinese garden art and attributed to the abundance of colorful landscape resources in the country.

According to historical record, rock collection was a sophisticated hobby for gentlemen scholars as early as the Spring and Autumn Period (770–476 B.C.). The use of rock in the Chinese garden can be traced back to the Sui dynasty (A.D. 590–617). The love of rock came into vogue during the Tang dynasty. For example, gardens in the city of Changan used mostly large river rocks hauled from the north side of the mountain Zhongnan Shan. The Zhongnan rocks were described as being hard, rounded, and waterwashed with grains of yellow and amber. Aesthetically, these rocks possessed the qualifications for artistic display. They were best arranged in solitary presentations with plants, or scattered in group compositions, rather than in piles. These compositions can be seen in the antique paintings of Wang Wei of the Tang dynasty, or in other ancient paintings, as representing an unpretentious, simple beauty characteristic of that historical period's art.

This kind of rock arrangement style was transmitted to Japan. As the rocks available in Japan resembled the Chinese Zhongnan rock, the scattered arrangements of rocks — with their differing shapes and distances in balanced compositions — gained prominence as a style of rockery art in Japan and eventually evolved as a singular art presentation to the world.

Collecting rocks had been an extravagant hobby and social vanity throughout ancient China's long history. Rocks of high artistic value were even given ranks, the way people are given titles of honor for their achievements. During the Northern Song dynasty (A.D. 960–1126), the imperial court sent out emissaries in search of exotic rocks and flowers to embellish the palatial garden. Rocks were brought from long distances, sometimes from hundreds of miles away. The famous ancient Chinese novel *The Outlaws of the Marsh* is based on the hardship that people had to endure while transporting grotesque rocks and exotic flowers to enrich the emperor's collections. The tallest monolithic rockery, measuring 6½ meters, the Crest-Cloud Peak (fig. 6.16) was moved into Suzhou's Liu Yuan, the Lingering Garden, over a thousand years ago during the Song dynasty. Flanked by two complementary monolithic rockeries, the Emerging-Cloud Peak and the Blessing-Cloud Peak, it comprises one of the most celebrated views of the garden (plan 3).

Du Wan of the Song dynasty edited the *Yuan Lin Catalog of Rocks,* which includes 116 different types of rocks. Contemporaneously, two outstanding styles of rock compositions had developed in the southern gardens, which include the graceful and elegant light-gray lake rock and the sturdy and staid yellow mountain rock, each with its own individual style. The lake rock was the highly prized variety quarried from the shores and bottom of Tai Hu, a lake in eastern China near the cities of Suzhou and Wuxi in Jiangsu Province. It is limestone eroded by water waves, with irregular shapes and sculptured cavities and holes. The corrugated, rough texture of the rock surface, with different shades of gray, adds to its elegance. The aesthetic criteria established for excellence are that the rock be "perforated, slender, and corrugated." The monolithic rockery strangely resembles contemporary sculpture with its abstract outline and positive and negative volumes (fig. 6.17). Therefore, it

FIG. 6.18 (top right) *The Summer Hill in Qe Yuan, Yangzhou.*

FIG. 6.19 (bottom right) *Slatelike rocks are used to build an artificial hill in the Studio of Mental Peace in Beihai Park, Beijing. Its horizontal expression harmonizes well with the ascending walking gallery.*

became comprehensible to the occidental world only after the advent of abstract sculpture in modern times.

As the grains on the lake rock surface were neither horizontal nor vertical, but rather curved, the rocks could be displayed singly or piled and bound into a stately and lofty composition (fig. 6.18). The sculptural composition of a rockery is based on the shape and physical characteristics of its rocks. In binding the rocks into a group composition, the manipulation of the surface grains is crucial to achieving a natural look. The rocks' adjoining seams should be hidden among the grains.

The yellow rock appears more geometrical and angular in form (figs. 6.1, 6.12). As it is available within almost all the territories of China, yellow rock compositions are extensively used. These arrangements are characterized by an air of majestic magnificence. The artificial hill of yellow rock in the garden Yu Yuan, Shanghai, is famous for being the largest and the aesthetically best of all yellow rock presentations (fig. 6.1).

Most gardens are limited to one kind of rock. If there is a need for mixing several kinds of rock, it is advisable that they not be arranged within the same sight range. The garden Ge Yuan, Yangzhou, was composed of four kinds of rocks, showing four different rock hill scenes that represented the four seasons of the year (plan 8). The lake rock of the "summer hill" adjoined the yellow rock of the "autumn hill." In order to minimize the unnatural-looking mixture of different rocks, the rockery display was lowered in elevation at the joining point and formed flower beds with selected lake rocks of yellowish tint and yellow rocks of grayish tint. This achieved a harmonious transitional appearance.

Formation of the above-mentioned more popular rock hill styles involved special techniques, mastered by special artisans. Manuals were prepared for reference; one was the *Yuan Lin Catalog of Rocks.* Rock compositions with original styles were created based on the individual character of various rocks. The rock hills in Ban Yuan, A Half Garden, in Beijing, were composed of local slatelike green rocks. Since the shape of the rock would not fit into the mold of tall, vertical rock hills, horizontal compositions were sculptured in medium height, embellished with decorative holes, contrasted with tall, upright trees. This novel approach provides a unique focal point for this representative garden of the north. Another rockery composed of slatelike rocks is in the garden of a palace for a Qing dynasty prince, Gong-Huang-Fu, in Beijing. The rockery's horizontal composition harmonizes wonderfully with the ascending walking gallery (fig. 6.19).

Despite the presence of numerous architectural structures, the Chinese garden still prevails as a naturalistic landscape. The magic touch of its artificial hills accomplishes this miracle. The artificial hill and rockery structure, half natural and half crafted by masons, serve as transitions from constructed artifacts to the naturalistic landscape settings. With a limited quantity of plant life in Chinese gardens, rockery and artificial hill symbolically represent naturalistic landscape with dramatic effect. Rockery displays in garden scenes have the advantage over plantings of producing an instant visual effect after construction. Moreover, they seldom require maintenance work. As for the plant

life, it may not gain full appreciation until its maturity at a later date. Thus, the artificial hill and rockery presentations possess all the fascinating qualifications that are necessary for becoming essential garden features in the Chinese Garden.

Management of Water

Water was as important in creating moods and emotional appeal in the garden as eyes are in the human face. In founding a garden in ancient China, sources of water were the essential site-selecting factor, instigated by Chinese geomancy, *feng-shui,* which prophesied wealth wherever water is found. A generous expanse of placid water—in the form of ponds or lakes with irregular shapes and in a varied composition of hills and other components—is a central feature that lends serenity to gardens of different sizes (fig. 1.5). Even a tiny pool can be a beloved attraction in compact areas (fig. 6.20). The watercourt in the Unsuccessful Politician's Garden, defined by the roofed bridge, the Little Flying Rainbow, and waterside pavilions and walking galleries, is a unanimously celebrated example (plan 1, fig. 6.21).

Different ways of playing with reflection of water greatly contribute to the individual garden's intended character (fig. 6.22). A water pavilion commanding water scenes in different directions (fig. 6.23), boatlike house berthing by a corner of a larger pond (fig. 6.24), walking galleries meandering along the embankment (fig. 6.25), and pavilions of differing forms dispersed along the waterside are typical water scenes of Chinese gardens. A body of water most effectively unifies the garden by focusing the observer's attention on itself as well as on the features around it.

Besides, water is the only garden component that does not constrict space. On the contrary, its mirroring effect enhances the sense of spaciousness. Another unique significance of the watercourse is that it serves as the "void space" in a traditional Chinese painting. A fairly large area of a painting may be left unpainted. The unpainted area is by no means less important than the painted objects in the pictorial composition. The entire composition might be balanced by a verse in the "void space," written in artistic calligraphy and commenting on the depicted subject. The composition could be offset by a vermilion print of an artistically designed stamp placed in the corner of the painting to define the void space.

Thus, the water surface in a Chinese garden is often found boldly dominating an area exceeding more than a half of the entire garden under the same principle as traditional painting. To be precise, in Beijing's Summer Palace and Beihai Park, water surfaces dominate up to three-fourths and two-thirds of their plots, respectively, (plans 14.A, 15). As for the Unsuccessful Politician's Garden in Suzhou (plan 1), the central pond occupies three-fifths of the total garden area and over 80 percent of the buildings were constructed along the watercourses.

The water in a garden is not intended merely to be enjoyed from a distance but to provide the delightful experience of being surrounded by water. Isles, promontories, and spits were incorporated wherever the size of the pond made it possible (fig. 6.26).

FIG. 6.20 (top left) *The embankment of the small pool in the garden Canglang Ting, the Surging-Wave Pavilion, Suzhou, was built in tiers. Walking galleries attached to the boundary walls undulate with the land form. A pavilion for displaying a tablet inscribed with a Qing dynasty emperor's calligraphy is shown in the background.*

FIG. 6.21 (bottom left) *The celebrated water court in Zhuozheng Yuan, the Unsuccessful Politician's Garden, Suzhou, is defined by a roofed bridge, the Little Flying Rainbow.*

FIG. 6.22 (top right) *Water scene in Jichang Yuan, Carefree-Abiding Garden, looking toward Zhiyu Ting, Knowing-Fish Pavilion, Wuxi.*

FIG. 6.23 (right)   *A pavilion hanging over the pond in the Summer-Retreating Mountain Villa, Chengde. The embankment is constructed of earth and spotted with rocks.*

FIG. 6.24 (bottom left)   *A boatlike house berthing at a corner of the pond in Guyi Yuan, the Ancient Magnificent Garden, Shanghai.*

FIG. 6.25 (bottom right)   *A double gallery meanders along the canal surrounding the garden; Surging-Wave Pavilion, Suzhou.*

The island may simply be decorative piles of rocks, forming an inaccessible garden scene (fig. 6.27). Bridges or causeways are laid for passages to the island, varying with the size of the watercourse (figs. 6.28, 6.29). An open pavilion built on an island, or the tip of a promontory, is aesthetically effective as both a motif and a vantage point for water scenes in all directions. To allow closer contact with the water, small bridges of single planks of stone, placed lower than the embankment in a precarious manner, allow the beholder to experience the thrill of an adventure in the wilderness. Stepping stones of various designs are favored for the amusement of crossing right over the meandering ripples (fig. 6.30). Decorative steps leading down to the water surface promote direct contact with the water (fig. 6.31), with limbs dipping into the refreshing pond suggesting meditation.

The designing measures should vary with the situation of the water to achieve the best results. Smaller pools make a compact courtyard appear more spacious. They are usually simply girded with rocks or plants of limited growth to retain a mirroring water surface for full reflection of the bright sky (fig. 6.22). Large central ponds are often shaded by tall deciduous trees with dark foliage to create a refreshing, cool atmosphere in the summer (fig. 6.32). Supreme peacefulness is expected from reflections of light-gray rockery and a segment of whitewashed plastered walls (fig. 6.25). During the winter, the bright sunshine filtered through bare twigs reflects warmth and cheerfulness in the garden. In larger gardens, old evergreen trees are planted to cast dark shadows on part of the central pond, contrasting with the bright reflections of the pond's exposed portion.

In managing water surface, it is crucial that the size of the reflected object be proportionate to the reflecting pond and be placed as close to the water surface as possible to obtain a complete reflection (fig. 6.33a). When the object, such as a sizable hall, happens to be out of proportion with the reflecting water surface, it is wise to set it back from the waterfront by building a terrace next to the water. Plants and rocks displayed between buildings and watercourses serve as transitions that mend the incomplete reflections of the recessed objects (fig. 6.33b).

The Chinese garden maker took painstaking efforts to ensure that the water level was maintained up to the edge of the embankment in order to combine the space over the pond with the space surrounding it. An abrupt change in the level of the ground and water surfaces tends to break up the continuity of space, ruining the pond's perspective and sometimes giving it the appearance of an uninteresting water well. This method of handling water obtains a full reflection of the sky and the garden scenes along the pond. Besides, it gives the exquisitely designed architecture a fascinating floating effect (fig. 6.34).

The Surging-Wave Pavilion garden is dominated by rockery scenes, very uncommon in existing Chinese gardens (plan 5). A small pool is located at the east end beside a raised walking gallery. The embankment of the pool is artistically terraced to avoid a well-like appearance and also to provide plantings at different levels (fig. 6.20). Ancient garden makers took the abundance of water resources into serious consideration in selecting sites, but it was impossible for them to foresee the change in water level hundreds of years

FIG. 6.26 (top left) *A promontory, in the lake of the Ancient Magnificent Garden, Shanghai, greatly adds to the depth of the water scene.*

FIG. 6.27 (top right) *Piles of rocks are used to form an inaccessible water scene in Tongzhu Si, a temple in Kunming, Yunnan Province.*

FIG. 6.28 (bottom) *A narrow plank stone bridge, leading to a winding path, is lowered to meet the water surface to provide precarious excitement for the tourists.*

FIG. 6.29 (opposite, top left) *The Seventeen-Arch Bridge leads to the South Lake Isle in the lake Kunming Hu, in the Summer Palace, Beijing.*

FIG. 6.30 (opposite, top right) *A pathway of minimum width meanders along and descends to a pond.*

FIG. 6.31 (opposite, bottom left) *Steps leading down to the water surface provide direct contact with the water as well as being decorative.*

FIG. 6.32 (opposite, bottom right) *Lake rocks were favored in constructing the embankment in Yi Yuan, the Pleasure Garden, Suzhou.*

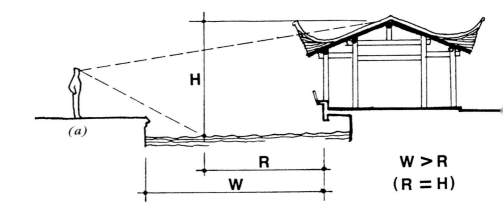

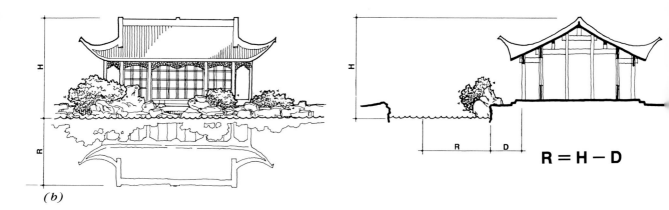

$W > R$
$(R = H)$

$R = H - D$

(b)

FIG. 6.33 (top) *Water and reflection:* a. *relationship between the reflecting pool and the object being reflected;* b. *treatment mending the incomplete reflection of recessed objects.*

FIG. 6.34 (bottom) *The Hut for Retreat and Meditation, with an exquisite floating effect, in Tesi Yuan, the Retreat and Meditate Garden, Suzhou.*

later. Therefore, quite a few existing ancient gardens present uninteresting water scenes with lowered water levels (fig. 6.35).

Besides the celebrated leitmotiv of a large, concentrated body of water, linear water surface—in the form of poetic "streamlet with a tiny bridge" leading away from a pond—is a much favored approach in managing the water inlet or outlet of the garden (figs. 6.36, 6.37). The enormous yellow stone artificial hill in Yu Yuan, Shanghai, is the predominant view of the garden. A stream meanders along the valley of the hill leading from the reflecting pond (plan 12). This is another successful theme in water management incorporated with artificial hills, praised as the "water meandering along the hills and hills enlivened by the water."

The excitement of exuberant running water is attractive to the Chinese taste; however, to be consistent with the unifying tranquillity of the garden, waterfalls are often molded into a remote recess of artificial hills. The waterfall's descent is carefully constructed with rocks that create fascinating sights. To make the view more appealing and natural, the gracefully manipulated cascade is often half screened by vegetation.

When water supply was totally absent in a garden site, rainfall water was collected from the gutters of nearby buildings to fill small ponds or create a waterfall. Such waterfalls are attractive even during the dry seasons since the water stains on the artistically manipulated rockery are competitive with real waterfalls. This is the so-called method of "water scene in dry form."

The formation of a pond takes up a major part of the garden construction work. Therefore, despite the seemingly extravagant utilization of rocks in Chinese gardens, the embankments of watercourses were treated with indifference for aesthetic and economic reasons. Relevant to the molding of artificial hills, there are three basic types of embankment construction found in Chinese gardens.

The first type is rock construction. Among different kinds of rock-girding embankments, lake rock is particularly loved for sculpturing artistic shorelines. The porous rocks with irregular shapes were often constructed as overhanging structures, producing the illusion of a larger water surface. Therefore, the perforated lake rocks are particularly suited for construction of small ponds in courtyard gardens (fig. 6.31).

Natural stonework, artistically manipulated, prevails in most of the stone embankments; but the ashlar stone embankment was sometimes constructed as the matching continuation of a terrace or the base of waterside buildings (fig. 6.38). Different kinds of stonework may be found in the same embankment. The joints of different treatments are made inconspicuous by screens made of plants; they are discontinued by the intersection of a bridge or by the application of other garden features used as transitions. As for the large ponds, stone embankments of lake rocks, yellow rock, or other kinds of rock are very expensive. Also, it requires sophisticated taste and crafting skill to achieve a satisfactory presentation; otherwise, such masonry tends to appear overelaborate and unnatural.

The second type of embankment construction is earth-rock combination, most often carried out as an earth bank sparsely spotted with rocks (fig. 6.23).

FIG. 6.35 (top left)   *A pavilion in Ou Yuan, the Lotus Root Garden, Suzhou. The surrounding loggia functions as both spatial transition and weather protection. Unfortunately, the esthetic quality of this pavilion suffers from the lowered water level of the pond.*

FIG. 6.36 (top right)   *A streamlet between rockeries leads to a hidden water source in Jixiao Shanzhuang, the Roar-Resounding Mountain Villa, Yangzhou.*

FIG. 6.37 (bottom left)   *A corner of a pond is defined by a crooked bridge, lending an air of intimacy, in Zhuozheng Yuan, the Unsuccessful Politician's Garden, Suzhou.*

FIG. 6.38 (bottom right)   *Ashlar stone base of the pavilions in Bishu Shanzhuang, the Summer-Retreating Mountain Villa, Chengde, Hebei Province, forms part of the pond's embankment.*

This type of bank construction is both aesthetically pleasing and economic in construction, but it has one drawback: The pattern of rock distribution should not be evenly repeated. The group composition of rocks and control of the distance between groups of rocks should be manipulated with good taste. The combined use of soil and rock in embankment construction is desirable because the amount of rock can vary according to availability, but the technique of manipulating rocks and plantings artistically is crucial to the success of a performance.

The third type of embankment is made with soil. For large watercourses, the earth bank is more practicable; it uses a variety of plants to create naturalistic water scenes. An interesting ambiguity between the water and land is often created by continuous planting of land plants and aquatic plants along the soil embankments.

Natural springs were often introduced as water resources for garden ponds. Wells were dug deep enough to connect watercourses with an underground water source to assure a water supply during the dry seasons. The temperature of well water, cool during summer and warm during winter, is desirable for the cultivation of golden carps. Some ponds in the gardens were connected with rivers, and some gardens were devised with floodgates to control the water level.

The watercourse, much loved and extensively applied in Chinese gardens, is not merely for aesthetic reasons. Physically, it absorbs the heat and adjusts the microclimate during the warmer seasons. Moreover, its presence assures the magnificence of incomparable serenity in Chinese gardens.

CHAPTER SEVEN
Architecture

Architecture predominates over plant life in the Chinese garden scene. This main emphasis differs greatly from that of western gardens. In most western garden design books, architecture is not even taken as a component; but in the ancient Chinese garden manual *Yuan Ye,* the longest chapter discusses the importance of architecture in the garden, while plants are only discussed along with other elements, without a special chapter. Anyone who first visits a Chinese garden, with a naturalistic landscape garden in mind, will no doubt be very astonished to find an extraordinary number of buildings. It is quite accurate to say that a garden in the Occident is planted but a Chinese garden is built.

In China, a series of genuine garden architectures evolved and crystallized through thousands of years of practice. A large variety of building types were developed to fit particular situations in the garden as well as to facilitate daily and occasional needs of habitation. Each building type has an appealing individually characteristic form of its own — with special size, proportion, and details that yield to modification without losing their individuality.

The disposition and design of garden architecture are guided by dual criteria: architecture functions both as a viewing-point and as part of the garden scene. When the hill-and-water landscape scene serves as the center of interest in a garden, viewing points are likely to be arranged in dedicated buildings. These buildings serve, in turn, as pictorial components of the garden view and are, therefore, subject to being channeled as vistas from other viewing points. The central garden in the Unsuccessful Politician's Garden is an excellent example (plan 1). Each of its buildings, set along the central pond, serves as *dui-jing,* opposing vista or counterpoint, to other buildings from different directions as well as viewing points (plan 1).

Instead of integrating the accommodations for various functional needs in a massive and stately building complex — as in western architectural traditions — Chinese traditional architecture presents smaller sized buildings in group compositions that incorporate courtyards (fig. 7.1). Chinese garden architecture is also presented in clustered buildings, but it differs from the formal symmetrical architectural tradition by excelling in romantic and asymmetric layout and design (fig. 7.2). Larger mansions, *lou,* are often treated with segmented design to avoid an overpowering effect. That is why clustered pavilions, rhythmically positioned, are conspicuous and spectacular in their total volume while the smaller size of individual pavilions sets off the vastness of the garden space (fig. 7.3). With these ingenious methods, Chinese garden architecture, despite its enormous quantity, serves as one of the components — or sometimes merely the backdrop — to the garden scenes of rockeries and plants (fig. 5.2).

The traditional post-and-beam timber structure endows the buildings with intricate form and shapes, including extremely decorative curved roofs. The weighty roofs, structurally designed for resisting wind lift, are made visually lighter by means of dramatically upturned eaves. These roofs rest on extraordinarily slender timber posts; and with the presence of solid stone platforms, these buildings have a floating but fantastically stabilized appearance (fig. 6.23). Functionally, the deep cantilever of the eaves provides adequate shelter for rain and scorching summer sun; the upturning allows the slanting winter sunlight to penetrate the building. Besides, as no gutter is provided in

FIG. 7.1 *(a) The western architectural tradition — a stately building complex; (b) the Chinese architectural tradition — smaller buildings in group composition.*

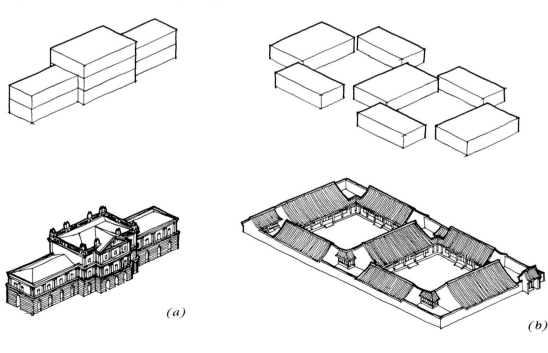

(a)

(b)

FIG. 7.2 (above)   *Fu Zhuang, Wild Ducks Village, along the Slender West Lake, a scenic spot in Yangzhou, Jiangsu Province, was built as a picturesque group composition of various building types and courtyards.*

FIG. 7.3 (left)   *The Five Dragon Pavilions in Beihai, the North Sea Park, present a spectacular water scene in group composition.*

FIG. 7.4 (above) *View from the Bright Zither Mansion to the hill and water scene of the main scenic section in the Lingering Garden, Suzhou.*

FIG. 7.5 (right) *A view of a courtyard in Hanshan Si, the Humble Hill Temple, Suzhou. The walking gallery is connected to the hall, with a loggia as the space transition. Southern magnolias are favorite plantings in courtyards beside halls.*

traditional Chinese architecture, upturning of the eaves also functions to thrust the rain further away from the building and thus avoid unpleasant and damaging splashings on the timber structure.

Garden architecture, in general, takes the form of open shelters and defines space from overhead without blocking up the continuity of space. The posts and beams of the open shelters serve as picture frames that focus and greatly enhance the magnificence of garden scenes (fig. 7.4). Buildings intended for habitation are usually fenestrated on all sides to give a lightened appearance and to command garden views in all directions (fig. 5.6). Walls are applied to control directional viewing from the building and to add aesthetically to its appearance (fig. 6.35).

Much effort was taken to organize the garden space into orderly sequences of enclosed, sheltered, and open-air sections. That is, the continuity of indoor and outdoor space was retained by gradual transition (fig. 3.3). An open walking gallery was hardly ever joined directly to an enclosed edifice without a loggia as a transition (fig. 7.5). All these artistic garden architecture design principles contribute to the unity of space throughout the garden.

Since a large quantity of architecture and a great variety of building types are indispensable to Chinese gardens, architecture serves as a unifying medium in disposing the space of the garden entity. There is no Chinese garden devoid of architecture, and there is no way to eliminate architecture from a typical Chinese garden scene.

Building Types

Main hall, tīng *or* tang *(fig. 7.6)*   *Tīng* or *Dong,* the main hall, is a sizable structure with a comparatively lofty space occupying a key position as the accent of the garden composition and the center for activities held in the garden. It was asserted in *Yuan Ye:* "In founding a garden, the disposition of the main hall is essential; it is to be south-oriented and located in a position to command the dominating garden scene." The southern orientation of main buildings in all traditional Chinese architecture, including *tīng* or *tang* in Chinese gardens, is strongly stressed up to the present day. The origin of this

FIG. 7.6   *The Distant Fragrance Hall, the main hall of the Unsuccessful Politician's Garden, has a spacious terrace as a transition to the central pond.*

practice is related to Chinese geomancy; *feng-shui* came, in fact, from the practical needs of improving the building's physical condition. According to the geographical conditions in most parts of China, southern orientation affords the most convenient sun exposure and natural ventilation during different seasons. A south-oriented building also presents a delightful sunlit appearance.

To cope with formal parties and the celebration of special occasions and festivals, the main hall usually has a relatively formal appearance and is often referred to as the *hua-ting*, flower hall, to distinguish it from the main hall of the traditional courtyard house. A flower hall could be fenestrated on all sides or walled on two or three sides to cope with the scenic dispositions around it. When viewing is desirable on all sides, convertible full-length windows are preferred. Taking the window panels off provides extra fluidity of air and sight lines. Loggias of differing width and design are employed to ensure extra protection from slanting rainfall during windstorms. The loggia also serves as a transition from the indoor space of the hall to the open-air space (fig. 6.35).

A terrace is often found in front of a sizable hall along the central pond to provide the enjoyment of open air viewing as a change from viewing from the hall. Terraces are also important as transitions between sizable halls and ponds (fig. 7.6). They give a lowered reflected image of the hall and keep the smaller pool from being dwarfed by the overpowering mass of the hall. Main halls in Chinese gardens are designed to be predominant but not overpowering. It is most important that a building, especially a large one, be positioned in an appropriate relationship to other garden features.

Pavilion, tíng   The pavilion, small in size and varied in form, is the basic and ubiquitous feature of the Chinese garden. The word *tíng,* which originated phonetically from a Chinese word meaning "stop," clearly indicates its function as a rest stop. Being light and open, the pavilion acquires the ideal form of garden architecture, is interspersed with scenic views, blends well into the naturalistic landscape, and, at the same time, serves as a sheltered vantage point commanding views in all directions. Pavilions are usually built free-standing on a hillside (fig. 7.7), half hidden in groves or a rockery (fig. 6.1), or on the watercourse (fig. 7.8). They can be cut in half, connected with galleries, and attached to a wall (fig. 7.9). The plan of a pavilion can be square, rectangular, hexagonal, octagonal, circular, fan-shaped, or any shape selected by the designer.

The roof further contributes to the structure's fascinating appearance with its vast variety of shapes and styles. Pyramidal, conical, hipped, half-hipped and half-gabled roofs are the most popular. The double-tiered pavilion with its intricate form is the summit of architectural decorativeness in the imperial gardens (figs. 7.10, 7.11).

The lightness of the pavilion in Chinese gardens — the "floating here and there" effect — is achieved the same way as in other building types but to a higher degree, by simply allowing the weighty tiled roof to rest on slender wooden posts. The benchlike balustrades accommodate stop-and rest needs, structurally tying the posts and providing stability, aesthetically, as well.

FIG. 7.7 (top left)   *The Bamboo Hat Pavilion in the Unsuccessful Politician's Garden is half hidden in groves on an artificial hill; it serves as a garden view and as a raised viewing point.*

FIG. 7.8 (top right)   *A pavilion built along a pond in the Crooked Court of Breeze and Lotus, West Lake, Hangzhou.*

FIG. 7.9 (center left)   *A half pavilion attached to a wall emphasizes an entryway.*

FIG. 7.10 (center right)   *An elaborate pavilion in an imperial garden, Zhongshan Gongyuan, Dr. Sun Yat-sen's Park, Beijing, with double-circular plan and double-tiered roof.*

FIG. 7.11 (bottom)   *A pavilion with intricately designed plan and roof, in the Summer-Retreating Mountain Villa, Chengde.*

FIG. 7.12 (above left) *A crooked gallery attached to a wall pierced with trellis windows. A flight of steps leads to a secondary touring route; in the Surging-Wave Pavilion garden, Suzhou.*

FIG. 7.13 (above right) *The most romantic walking gallery, along a partition wall in the inner garden of the Unsuccessful Politician's Garden, undulating horizontally and vertically upon the water. Wherever the gallery angles away from the wall, a tiny court is formed for a scenic presentation.*

FIG. 7.14 (right) *A double walking gallery in Yi Yuan, the Pleasure Garden, Suzhou. The trellis windows on the center wall of the gallery reunite the divided space.*

It is advisable not to build a pavilion on the summit of a hill for fear of dwarfing the hill, with a resulting uninteresting effect. According to a Chinese garden design principle, total exposure of the garden views exhausts the viewer's initiative to explore further. When looking from a pavilion built on a declining slope, one has a panoramic view in one direction; the other side remains to be visited later or on a second trip.

In the Imperial Palace, Beijing, five pavilions were erected symmetrically on the ridge of Jing Shan, the Viewing Hill, forming a singular silhouette against the changing sky. This is an exceptional example of pavilions with an air of magnificence, instead of the subtle grace usual in private gardens. Pavilions on the Viewing Hill also have panoramic views of the Imperial Palace, a special feature owing to the emperors' desire to have their territory completely under their command.

Walking gallery, **long**   The walking gallery is a spectacular reappearing feature that connects garden buildings; it also serves as a space-confining device. While dividing, it unites the different scenic sections by being open and unobstructive (fig. 5.11), greatly adding to the depth and sequence of the garden views. The walking-gallery tends to be long and crooked (fig. 7.12), undulates horizontally and vertically with the land contour, and ascends freely upon a hill or flies dramatically over a watercourse (fig. 7.13). Its design can be free-standing, attached to a wall, or it can take the form of a double gallery with a wall built along the center line (fig. 7.14). As regards location, it can be built along the garden's boundary wall or as an internal partition. Two-story walking galleries were built in Ge Yuan, Yangzhou, to provide innovative, elevated touring routes (fig. 6.13). Connected with paths and bridges, the gallery is a prime garden touring route and a most spectacular building type in the Chinese garden.

Water pavilion, **shui-xie** *(fig. 7.15)*   Water pavilions and the boatlike houses are special types of building structures arranged along the watercourse for the highlighting and enjoyment of water scenes. The water pavilion is mostly oblong, with its longer and open side projecting onto the watercourse. Its waterside facade is usually fully lined with wooden balustrades or a long settee, called the "beautiful lady's recliner," for enjoying the lotus, the golden carps, the reflection of the moon in the pond, and various water scenes. Generally, the back of the water pavilion has a wall decorated with fancy doors, window openings, or ornamental wall hangings such as plaques or vertical panels. Water pavilion is one of the most romantic types of garden architecture, fulfilling aesthetic satisfaction by both its appearance and its function as a viewing point for water scenes.

Boatlike House, **Fong** *(fig. 7.16)*   The boatlike house is an ambiguous feature thrust onto the watercourse to create the imaginary experience of cruising on a pleasure boat (fig. 7.17). A deck is indispensable and is often built with a parlor and an anteroom; sometimes the building is raised in height at the rear for better viewing from the second floor. A famous example of the

FIG. 7.15 (above left)   *A water pavilion in Jichang Yuan, the Carefree-Abiding Garden, Wuxi.*

FIG. 7.16 (above right)   *A boatlike house, Xian Zhou, the Fragrant Island, in the Unsuccessful Politician's Garden, with a typical layout of its type, is an example of transition from open air to indoor space, in the order of: unsheltered "deck," sheltered porch, enclosed parlor, and multistory or single-story antechamber. The boatlike house is further enlivened by drooping vines.*

FIG. 7.17 (center)   *A boatlike house in an imperial garden, Tianwang Fu, Beijing. The roofs are characteristically different from the architectural style found in southern China: the eaves have a smaller cantilever, and the roof is less sloped.*

FIG. 7.18 (bottom)   *The white marble boat in the Summer Palace, Beijing, was built with an obvious influence of European baroque.*

FIG. 7.19 *Yangshan Tang,*
Looking Up to the Mountain
Hall, in Yu Yuan, the
Pleasing Garden, Shanghai, is
treated with segmented
design to avoid an
overpowering effect upon the
adjacent pond of limited area.

boatlike house was built by the Empress Dowager Cixi of the late Qing dynasty; she diverted funds from naval construction to build a white marble pleasure boat, one of the wonders of the Summer Palace in Beijing (fig. 7.18).

Mansion, lou *(fig. 7.19)*   Tall, sizable buildings are usually avoided in private gardens. Buildings were mostly limited to two stories, with diminished ceiling height, in order to maintain a proportional relation with the surrounding space and garden features. Two-story buildings are most often found in remote corners of the garden; this avoids overpowering the garden with building mass. The positive use of multistory buildings was to block out unpleasant sights adjoining the site or to provide elevated viewing points with a wider sight range for enjoying scenes of the garden or borrowed views of the vicinity.

Tower, ko *(fig. 7.20)*   *Ko* could be either one- or two-story but was always raised in position, sustaining a floating appearance, and most often fenestrated on four sides to provide viewing opportunities in different directions. *Lou* and *ko* were built with an indoor stairway or attached to an open-air rockery comprised of steps forming an adventurous access to the second floor.

Stage, xi-tai *(fig. 7.21)*   Stages of various sizes and designs are found in gardens built in Ming and Qing dynasties. Stages are mentioned here not only as a building type but as an example of how sizable structures with more

FIG. 7.20 (right)   *Kuai Lou, the Tower of Joy, in Yu Yuan, Shanghai, built on a rocky hill, is, in fact, a ko. Small as it is, it is called a* lou, *to suggest the idea of a "mansion." This gives the illusion of a large building as well as an enlarged image of the rocky hill. The upturned, elaborate roof is an expression of joy.*

FIG. 7.21 (below)   *The stage, the reflecting pond, and the "balcony" in the Roar-Resounding Mountain Villa, Yangzhou.*

complicated demands were handled in Chinese garden composition. The stage in the Roar-Resounding Mountain Villa, Yangzhou, was built in the form of a pavilion seemingly floating on a central pond. The water surface in front of it serves as a sound-reflecting device that adds to the acoustic effect of musical and theatrical performances. The two-story halls and galleries surrounding the compound take the place of the balcony in a proper theater. This celebrated garden illustrates an ingenious approach that fulfills utilitarian demands as well as being an aesthetic success. This garden eloquently suggests that great designers owe their success to the challenge of their project's particular requirements. The three-story stage in the Summer Palace, Beijing — elaborate in ornamentation and gigantic in size — stands unique among all stages of the world by allowing simultaneous performances on three different floors.

Other buildings   Some garden buildings bear special names only because of their usage or location not their architectural characteristics. A *zhai* is a secluded house used for cultural activities or religious purposes. A sizable building for temporary living or use as a guest house was called *guan*. A *xuan* is a building with a lofty space for habitation, usually situated at a location offering a perspective of garden scenes. These buildings are often found in remote spots such as inner gardens; they are ideal places for meditation and serious cultural activities. Static views, meant for long-term, close-up observation, were provided as a refreshing change from hard mental work.

Thus, a great variety of Chinese garden architecture originated to enrich garden scenes as well as to provide vantage points. In spite of all the specific names the building types bear and their significant identities in form, size, proportion, and detail, alterations are allowed to the extent that each building type retains its individuality. With the creation of numerous building types, ample architectural vocabulary is afforded to cope with the composition of multifarious garden scenes. The unlimited imagination of ancient Chinese garden makers resulted in even more innovative architectural structures. Some are hard to categorize as specific building types but are as attractive as ever: for example, bridges surmounted by pavilions or walking galleries of various designs (figs. 6.21, 7.22). The ancient Chinese garden makers were ingenious in presenting timber structure with a unified style, characterized as being light, exquisite, and ornamental, with a sense of transparency.

Courtyards (fig. 7.23)

The courtyard is a basic form of spatial design in the Chinese garden that accommodates more confined and secluded scenic sections and is most effective in creating serene environments with varied moods and atmospheres. Courtyards can also be inserted as transitional space between architectural complexes.

Generally, courtyards can be classified by size into three types: medium-sized, small, and larger. Medium-sized courtyards are often built in front and

FIG. 7.22 *A walking gallery,*
mounting over a bridgelike
rockery, divides the
watercourse without blocking
the space; in the Unsuccessful
Politician's Garden, Suzhou.

at the back of more important halls enclosed by buildings and or walls on the other sides. Much praised examples are the Magnolia Hall in the Unsuccessful Politician's Garden (plan 1), the Five-Peak Immortal Hall in the Lingering Garden (fig. 7.23A), Bowing-to-the-Rock Studio in the Pleasure Garden (fig. 7.23E), and the Five-Peak Studio in the Net Master's Garden (plan 2). These courtyards are all embellished with elaborate static views, to be discussed in Chapter Twelve. Most often, sizable rockeries are the dominating theme in the front courtyard, and a more spacious layout is applied at the back as a contrast, or vice versa (figs. 2.5, 7.24).

Small courts often flank a building or are placed to one side of a crooked walking gallery; amazingly small in area, they nevertheless excel in enchanting scenic compositions of diversified design (fig. 7.25). Small courts are also used for functional purposes such as lighting and ventilation, and they embellish individual rooms or building complexes (fig. 7.26). Some of them are designed as vistas or appear at turnings along walking galleries (fig. 7.27).

Scenic compositions in small courts are often limited to one or two spectacular arbor trees or a few stalks of bamboo. The nandina, waxy plum blossom, and plantain trees — complemented with a few pieces of rock — are other favorite focal points for these locations, creating a happy resemblance to three-dimensional paintings or enlarged *bonzai*. A sequential arrangement of

FIG. 7.23 *Plans of courtyards: (A) the Five-Peak Immortal Hall in the Lingering Garden, Suzhou, with courtyards of varied sizes on four sides; (B) the Renowned Hall of Swallows in the Lion Grove garden, Suzhou, with courtyards at the front and back; (C) the Spring Home of Begonia in the Unsuccessful Politician's Garden, Suzhou, fronting a larger courtyard and flanked by two tiny courts — all planted with begonias; (D) Ou Yuan, the Pot Garden, Suzhou, measuring only 10 by 15 meters, includes all the major garden features — a pond, rockery, bridges, plants, pavilion, and walking gallery; (E) Bowing-to-the-Peak Studio in the Lingering Garden, Suzhou, with a larger courtyard at the front and smaller courts at one side and the back (south of the larger courtyard is the Hut in the Stone Forest); (F) a garden of courtyards attached to a house in Suzhou; (G) a courtyard garden in front of a studio in a Yangbou house.*

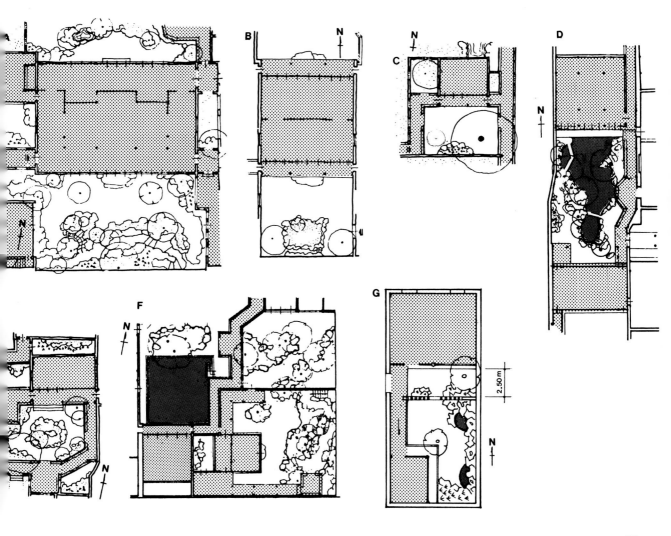

FIG. 7.24 (top left)   *A courtyard in front of a hall in the Roar-Resounding Mountain Villa, Yangzhou.*

FIG. 7.25 (top right)   *A tiny court in the Lingering Garden is embellished with a grove of bamboos that casts beguiling shadows on the whitewashed wall.*

FIG. 7.26 (bottom left)   *A tiny court in Tingfeng Yuan, the Listen to the Maple Garden, Suzhou, adorned as a window scene with rockery and plants.*

FIG. 7.27 (bottom right)   *A tiny court, formed by a crooked walking gallery and a wall, serves as a vista along the walking gallery; in the Surging-Wave Pavilion garden, Suzhou.*

smaller courtyards, often used, fosters an impression of depth and serenity in garden views (fig. 7.28).

Large courtyards are most often formed by groups of buildings, walking galleries, walls, rockeries, and plants, irregular in shape and diversified in design; they are more or less individually defined and yet usually incorporated with adjoining scenic sections as continuous space. A successful example is found in the Loquat Garden of the Unsuccessful Politician's Garden (plan 1). The exquisite space disposition around the Dainty Hall embellishes the hall with varied, harmonious views in different directions. An artificial hill screens the space at the northwest side but does not block scenic views from the garden's dominating scenic section.

Different types of courtyards can be characterized spatially as enclosed or open. Enclosed courtyards are relatively independent, exceedingly tranquil, and often accentuated by humble, yet elegant entry gates (fig. 7.29). As for spatial presentation, the interior space of enclosed courtyards tends toward having facades in four directions instead of a three-dimensional perspective. Thus, the courtyards are treated as "uncovered rooms," as most beguiling and ambiguous spaces expressing both the interior and the exterior (fig. 7.30).

The open-style courtyard is often defined by open walking galleries or walls with doors or window openings that ensure the fluidity of the space. This "borrowing" of space and views from adjoining scenic sections eliminates overconfinement. Thus, the composite use of a number of courtyards — in sequence or by surrounding a central courtyard with minor, smaller courts — is favored to further enrich the garden's spatial disposition. The Spring Home of Begonia in the Unsuccessful Politician's Garden has a front courtyard flanked by two smaller courts providing the hall with different views in four directions. The small courts are also devised to set off the spaciousness of the front court by contrast (fig. 7.23C). The Hut in the Stone Forest of the Lingering Garden is built with a large courtyard at the north and three small courts of strikingly differing shapes embracing the other sides (plan 3, item 26). Here, the group composition of the courtyards is further enhanced by being surrounded by more courts and yards of various design. This entire complex is a masterpiece of the composite use of courtyards.

Walls and Openings (fig. 7.31)

Walls in the Chinese gardens are not of the ordinary, blank, right-angled, functional masonry structure; they curve freely in plan, undulate vertically with the contour, or do both. Walls are presented as a most interesting and highly artistic element serving not only as boundaries and space dividers within the garden but also as essential screening devices in the art of concealing and revealing scenic interests. Walls further serve as backgrounds for garden scenes and to hide any unpleasant sights.

Walls can be found attached to walking galleries, pavilions, or rockeries (fig. 7.32). In order to blend well into the garden's naturalistic setting, the ends and joints of walls are hidden by other garden features such as plants or rockery (fig. 7.33).

FIG. 7.28 (top) *A small courtyard in the Lion Grove garden, Suzhou, is divided by a crooked walking gallery that greatly adds to the depth of the courtyard.*

FIG. 7.29 (center) *A pavilion built to embellish the entry of a courtyard in the Listen to the Maple Garden, Suzhou.*

FIG. 7.30 (bottom) *A small court in the Listen to the Maple Garden is, in fact, an "uncovered room."*

FIG. 7.31 (opposite, top left) *A wall in Qiuxia Pu, the Autumnal Cloud Garden, Shanghai, with a begonia-blossom-shaped gate. The inscriptions on the fan-shaped plaque mean "appreciating serenity."*

FIG. 7.32 (opposite, bottom) *A double walking gallery is used as the boundary of the garden Canglang Ting, the Surging-Wave Pavilion, Suzhou. The double gallery, built with a whitewashed center wall, undulates along the surrounding canal. A rockery embankment was built to enliven the lengthy walking gallery. Two Chinese parasol trees are vertical features emphasizing the descending silhouette of the rockery.*

FIG. 7.33 (opposite, top right) *A moon gate, hidden in rockeries, leads to an inner garden of the Pleasure Garden, Suzhou.*

When it is desirable to separate two scenic sections entirely, wall enclosures are constructed. The most decorative door and window openings on the walls are the ever-successful connections of scenic sections achieved by *jie-jing*, borrowing views, or *lou-jing*, divulging views. Openings of various shapes enable beholders to glimpse a fragment of scenery in the courtyard beyond. This arouses their curiosity for further exploration (fig. 7.34). Thus, the garden's smaller scenic sections not only borrow space from neighboring sections—through these ornamental openings—but also attract the most careless viewer's attention to focal points of the enclosed scenery through "divulging views." The moon gate is a most dramatic feature, offering a "framed view" that shows off the garden scenes and makes anyone's first shot look professional.

A whitewashed wall with blue-black tiled roofing, with or without a low stone base (fig. 7.35), is the characteristic feature of the southern private garden; an ochre-red plastered wall roofed with golden-yellow or deep-green glazed tiles identifies the imperial garden in the north. Gray terra-cotta brick is another favorite for garden walls; often it is finely polished or ornamented with delicate carvings. Unremarkable when observed from a distance, its elegance and subtle crafting can be seen on close observation. Terra-cotta brickwork is also favored for framing door or window openings (fig. 7.33).

Partitions of natural materials, such as rubble stone walls and wood or bamboo fences, were recommended in the garden-building manual *Yuan Ye* and were often depicted in Chinese traditional paintings. Their rustic beauty was said to be in harmony with the intricacies of nature. Unfortunately, gardens existing today tend toward the elaborate Qing dynasty style, and the rustic beauty of simplicity, theoretically advocated, can scarcely be found.

One of the most spectacular wall types is the "cloud wall," which has a sine curve at the top (fig. 7.36). When the blue-black, curved, tiled roofing of an undulating cloud wall is decorated with a pattern resembling the scales of the legendary dragon, the immortal creature seemingly rests upon the winding wall. Gigantic dragon heads were sculptured upon the enclosure walls of the garden Yu Yuan in Shanghai and certain other gardens (fig. 7.37). Fire destroyed many timber structures in the history of Chinese architecture. The dragon was believed to be a guardian who protected buildings from fire by throwing water conveyed from the sea. The eye-catching "dragon wall" fascinates curious tourists with realistic tastes, but it is a later development that seems contradictory to the original refined and thought-provoking conceptions of traditional Chinese garden art.

With the likelihood of harsh reflection, the wall has seldom been found too close to the watercourse. Paths, rocks, and, more often, plant life—or at least a stone base—are placed between the water and the wall to procure a more vivid mirrored image (figs. 6.9, 7.32). A glimpse of whitewashed wall always pleasantly enlivens the sedate, dark reflection of a garden scene in a pond.

Wall-opening traceries are magnificently handicrafted with curved roof tiles or thin terra-cotta bricks as basic modular elements that offer an amazing variety of patterns (fig. 7.38*a* to *i*). Tracery can also be a clay-and-wire sculpture with geometric pattern, realistic scenes of landscape, animal figures, or

FIG. 7.34 (above left)   *The dominant water scene of Jichang Yuan, the Carefree-Abiding Garden, Wuxi, viewed through the window opening of a screening wall, presents a three-dimensional picture.*

FIG. 7.35 (center left)   *A wall in the Summer-Retreating Mountain Villa, Chengde, built with a rubble stone base.*

FIG. 7.36 (bottom left)   *A serpentine wall with a sine-curved top blends well with the natural curves of plant life; in the Unsuccessful Politician's Garden, Suzhou.*

FIG. 7.37 (above right)   *A "dragon wall" built to intersect a pathway winding up a hill adds to the depth of the scene viewed through an oval gate in Wei Shan Park, Wuxi.*

(a)

(b)

(c)

(d)

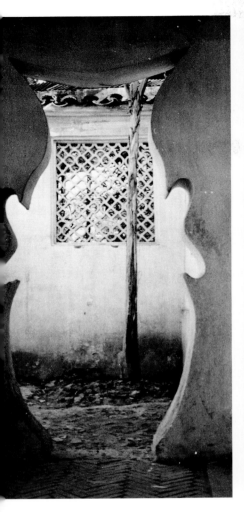

(i)

(f)

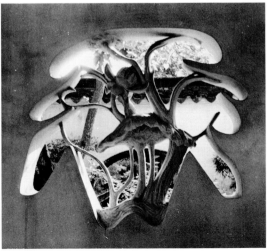

(h)

FIG. 7.38 *Wall-opening traceries: (a) window traceries constructed with curved roof tiles in the Lingering Garden, Suzhou; (b) window traceries constructed with thin terra-cotta bricks in the Lingering Garden; (c) a window tracery of geometric design, molded with clay and wire, in the Lingering Garden; (d) a clay-and-wire molded window tracery in Yi Yuan, the Pleasure Garden, Suzhou; (e) a gate in the shape of a flower vase leading to a small court; (f) looking into a small courtyard through a bottle-gourd-shaped door opening in the Surging-Wave Pavilion garden, Suzhou; (g) a pomegranate-shaped window opening mounted with tracery of a fruit-bearing peach tree molded of terra-cotta; (h) a plantlike, free-shape wndow opening mounted with molded lotus blossoms and leaves as the tracery; (i) a window tracery with a realistic design, a blissful scene of a peacock perching on a blooming peony, which symbolizes happiness and prosperity — in the garden of Qiongzhu Si, a temple in Kunming, Yunnan Province.*

even a scene from a famous opera legend. These more modern, realistic presentations were inconsistent with the wonderful implicitness of Chinese garden art tradition, but this is another indication that the Chinese garden is virtually a composite artwork integrated with various kinds of art and refined handicrafts.

Bridges (fig. 7.39)

The bridge, doing double duty, is carefully located and designed both to command a view of the water scene around it and as a decorative feature for the scenery. It is often erected along a touring route, giving diversity to the visitor who crosses a stream or gains access to an island. A bridge—often linked with a dike, a peninsula, or an island—can screen the rear part of a pond while allowing the viewer's eyesight to flow with the water under the bridge. Thus, the bridge is another important medium adding to the depth of the water scene, forming division not blockage. A bridge is often erected at the mouth of an inlet to conceal the supposed source of the water; it is also a vantage point for viewing a waterfall or a stream of extraordinary serenity leading to an imaginary fountain hidden in the woods (fig. 6.37). All this increases curiosity and urges viewers to continue further in their trip beyond the bridge.

Diversified forms of bridges in existing Chinese gardens are mostly made of stone with simple but elegant design or with intricately carved patterns congruent with their surroundings (fig. 7.39). The simple plank bridge is especially preferred for a small span of water in a confined area. Simplicity contributes to its continuity with the adjoining paved footpath (fig. 6.28). Occasionally, a bridge is accented by ornamental rocks or plant life at each end. Over the larger ponds, bridges are broken up into segments in a zigzag form for a better sense of scale. The zigzag bridge is favored not merely for its spectacular form but because it directs the eye to scenes arranged in different directions along the pond. Unsuccessful use of zigzag bridges in contemporary practice results from simply adopting the form without having changes of scene at the turnings (fig. 7.40); beholders thus complain of being compelled to travel the extra distance in vain.

A leveled bridge, either with a simple plank or in zigzag form, tends to be anchored lower than the bank in order to foster a sense of intimacy with the water. Its supporting posts are often hidden by the cantilevered beam-and-slab structure that gives the bridge a floating effect.

In lakes of vast area, ornamentation is often better than simplicity. Articulate forms and eye-catching bright colors produce dramatic effects. Bridges with gorgeous pavilions and even clusters of pavilions—such as the Five-Pavilion Bridge in the Slender West Lake, Yangzhou—are appreciated as scenery as well as for the enchanting picture frames that offset views in the vicinity (fig. 7.41).

When a pond or lake is large enough for boating, an arched bridge with a graceful curvature is often erected to permit a boat to pass under it. The arched bridge is a unique integration of structural and architectural beauty (fig. 7.39),

but its enchanting reflection in the water is only appropriate for a large span of water. The miniature arched bridge in the southeast corner of the Net Master's Garden in Suzhou is supposed to be an attraction of the famed garden (plan 2). Unfortunately, though the bridge is adjusted in scale to the proportions of the pond, it is out of scale with human size. Stepping onto the bridge, people feel as if they are intruding on a children's playground; they look to passersby like giants visiting a nation of midgets (fig. 7.42).

The railings of the bridges are designed with no less variety. Simple stone or steel-rod railing blends well with the naturalistic garden scene. The railing can be extraordinarily low for the purpose of providing a seat for enjoyment of the surrounding water scenes (fig. 6.37). Bridges with elaborately carved railings often fit into a more architectonic setting or become a continuation of the artifacts joining the naturalistic garden entity (fig. 7.39). The form and detail of bridges, like all other garden architecture, are designed to conform with the individual garden's general concept and the immediate surrounding context. Thus, innumerable types of bridges flourished in Chinese gardens.

Fenestration and Furniture (fig. 7.43)

Fenestration and furniture constitute the last but not the least items of garden architecture fulfilling utilitarian needs as well as expressing the particular environmental spirit anticipated by the garden owners.

Fenestration — windows, full-length doors, and railings — includes wooden carvings of designed patterns and exquisite crafting. An extensive collection of patterns for decorating fenestration as well as pavement is found in the ancient garden manual *Yuan Ye*. The existence of enormous wooden lattices noticeably lessens the light admitted, but the rooms are usually sufficiently lighted by the full fenestration between columns (figs. 7.44, 7.45). Like most artistic features of the Chinese garden, the magnificent lattice designs also originated functionally. Paper and extra thin mother-of-pearl plates, ground to translucence, took the place of present-day glass panes. The lattices were distributed densely, to protect the paper from the wind or to fit the small dimensions of the mother-of-pearl plates. A larger central panel was often added for viewing purpose once glass panes became available; the traditional lattice design was retained as ornamentation on the perimeter of the windows.

Full-length pivoting partitions provide flexibility of indoor space in the large buildings. They can be fully removed to convert rooms into a spacious hall for occasional activities. The partition wall panels were found mounted with traditional Chinese paintings and artistic calligraphy, or they were decorated with wood carvings (fig. 7.46a, b) and sophisticated handicrafts such as inlays of precious stone or mother-of-pearl. Stained glass is also used in later gardens built in Qing dynasty (fig. 7.47).

The full-length, pivoting windows enable a hall to be turned into a gigantic open pavilion during warmer seasons, further promoting unobstructed fluidity of space in the garden (fig. 7.48). When removable full-length windows

(a)

(b)

(c)

FIG. 7.43 *Furniture arrangements: (a) the Grace-Gathering Mansion in the Net Master's Garden, Suzhou — a gilded tablet inscribed with the title of the building, a gua-lao hung under the beam to emphasize the recessed space for the couch, furniture arranged in the style of a reception room; (b) formal furniture arrangement of a hall in Hanshan Si, the Humble Hill Temple, Suzhou; (c) Qing dynasty-style furniture with elaborate carving, in Qisheng Lou, the Chess-Winning Mansion, in Mochou Hu, Worry-Not Lake, Nanjing.*

(a)　　　　　　　　　　　　　　　　　　(b)

FIG. 7.44 (opposite, top left) *A view of full fenestrations between columns in the Surging-Wave Pavilion garden, Suzhou. The latticed members were densely distributed to protect the paper from wind pressure or to cope with the small dimensions of mother-of-pearl plates formerly used in place of glass panels.*

FIG. 7.45 (opposite, top right) *A latticed window in Hillside Immortal Music Hall in Yi Yuan, the Pleasure Garden, Suzhou.*

FIG. 7.46 (opposite, bottom) *Partitions: (a) full-length pivoting partition panels inscribed with paintings and artistic calligraphy; (b) the Respectables of the Forest and Fountains Hall in the Lingering Garden, Suzhou.*

FIG. 7.47 (top) *The Thirty-Six Mandarin Ducks Hall in the Unsuccessful Politician's Garden. Decorative wall panel partitions can be removed to unite two identical halls. Paintings are mounted on the removable partition wall panels. Stained glass is used extensively in this hall.*

FIG. 7.48 (center) *The full-length pivoting doors in Tesi Yuan, the Retreat and Meditate Garden, Suzhou.*

FIG. 7.49 (bottom) *View to the northeast from the Bright Zither Mansion in the Lingering Garden, Suzhou. A "beautiful lady's recliner," spanning the area between columns, and the gua-lao, hanging under the beams, make up an elaborate "picture frame" for the garden views.*

were installed, hanging over watercourses, extra wooden latticed railings were added on the outside for protection; this also improved natural ventilation and human comfort by admitting water-cooled breezes in the warm seasons (fig. 6.26). Moreover, the lattice design and craftsmanship greatly enhances the elegance of garden architecture.

Low railings of pavilions, galleries, and other types of buildings were intended to be used as elongated benches, for aesthetic pleasure and to accommodate the need for resting and viewing. The "beautiful lady's recliner" is another kind of ornamental railing; it functions as a sort of curved-back settee in which one's posture is romanticized as one sits and relaxes. It is also known as the "goose-neck settee" because the back curvature resembles the neck of a goose (fig. 7.49).

Bo-gu-jia, the curio-displaying shelf, is a special piece of built-in furniture serving as a decorative space partition in the form of shelves for curios or antique collections (fig. 7.50). The shelf divisions were artistically designed, greatly adding to the interior of the garden architecture. Choosing and arranging shelf displays is enjoyable and requires a refined taste.

Gua-luo, the hanging partition, is a most unique decorative feature hung under beams of conspicuous location, very effective in focusing a particular space (fig. 7.49). *Lou-di-zhao,* full-length screen, is another spectacular space-defining device; it serves no function of visual or sound insulation but adds greatly to the depth or spaciousness of a room. These ornamental features are usually installed at the central point of an informal hall to exhibit wood-carving art that excels in both design and craft (fig. 7.51*a, b*). Besides geometric patterns, realistic subjects are depicted so as to bring garden scenes into the building. Scenes of wisteria heavily loaded with blooming flowers and ripened grapevines with busy squirrels hopping around are a few of the favored subjects for the hanging partitions. Presentations were often so vividly executed by talented craftspeople that visitors could imagine themselves to be walking in an open-air garden under living grapevines or wisteria.

Stone tables, stools, and benches are displayed on terraces, in courtyards, or on the decks of the boatlike houses, to accommodate outdoor activities and be ornamental as well (figs. 7.52, 7.53). These refined masoncrafts are decorated with motifs or patterns that match the surrounding architectural molding of terraces, the bases of buildings, or the stone railings. Rocks in natural shape but with dimensions for different kinds of furniture use — such as a screen at a gate, a couch in a cave, or a table with stools on a terrace or on a rock hill — reproduce the romantic environment of primitive life (fig. 7.54).

Indoor furniture is found made of the same wooden material in patterns and paint that match the windows, doors, and interior partitions (figs. 7.43*b,* 7.46*a*). Different kinds of wood were used for furnishing different kinds of buildings. For instance, *hung-mu* and *tzu-t'an* were used in sumptuous buildings, while *nan-mu* and *huang-hua-li* were used for a touch of elegance. In the traditional gardens existing today, most of the furniture displayed is not original. Therefore, incongruities are obvious between furniture and architecture and also between pieces of furniture.

A singular style of furniture for garden architecture is made from gigantic

FIG. 7.50 (top) Bo-gu-jia, *curio-displaying shelf, in the anteroom of a remodeled reception room.*

FIG. 7.51 (bottom) *Screens: (a)* lou-di-zhao, *full-length screen, devised to accentuate an alcove in the hall in Ge Yuan, Yangzhou; (b) Full-length screen designed in the form of a moon gate.*

)

(b)

FIG. 7.52 (opposite, top)   *Outdoor furniture of a courtyard — stone tables, drum-shaped stools, and benchlike railing in Tingfeng Yuan, Listen to the Maple Garden, Suzhou, restored in 1985.*

FIG. 7.53 (opposite, bottom left)   *Stone tables and stools on the "deck" of the Pleasure Boat Studio in Yi Yuan, Suzhou; the low porch railing serves as benches.*

FIG. 7.54 (opposite, bottom right)   *Cement-molded table and stools in tree-trunk form built during the restoration of a Ming dynasty Garden, the Ancient Magnificent Garden, Shanghai.*

FIG. 7.55 (top)   *A couch with tea table made of roots and twisted branches; in the Surging-Wave Pavilion garden, Suzhou.*

FIG. 7.56 (bottom)   *A hall in the Listen to the Maple Garden with furniture of more succinct design. Ming dynasty armchairs are displayed beside the door in the photo. The tablet hung over the painting is inscribed with the name of the hall.*

FIG. 7.57 (top) *The pavement in a courtyard of the Slender West Lake, a scenic spot in Yangzhou. Pebbles of different colors are used in chessboard pattern. Bricks are used for highlighting. The border of the pavement is designed with a free-curved pattern that forms the transition to the lake rock flowerbed; in the Slender West Lake, Yangzhou.*

FIG. 7.58 (bottom) *Steps of natural rock and brick-paved paths provide access to the artificial hill; in the Summer Retreating Mountain Villa, Chengde.*

FIG. 7.59 (opposite) *Rocks, bricks, and other paving materials: (a) rocks used to construct flower beds, half buried in the ground, lend a natural look in the Slender West Lake, Yangzhou; (b) crushed stones and broken bricks utilized in patched pattern and roughly worked stone benches lend a rustic look to the Surging-Wave Pavilion, Suzhou; (c) crushed stones and broken bricks form the geometric pattern of a walkway; (d) pebbles and curved roof tiles form the favored begonia-blossom pattern; (e) pebbles, slates, curved roof tiles, and broken porcelain (the light color) form elaborate color patterns; (f) (bottom right) animal figures, crane and deer, auspicious symbols of longevity, are used as a pattern.*

(a)

(b)

(c)

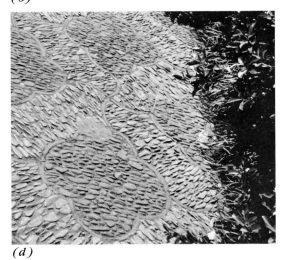

(d)

(e)

(f)

roots of trees. This also originated out of a love and imagination for life in the wilderness. It was romantic in concept and attractive for aesthetic enjoyment but generally not very comfortable (fig. 7.55).

Hardwood was used in furniture making back as far as the Ming dynasty. This enabled designers to use slender components. Ming dynasty furniture is rarely found in existing gardens. It is characterized by simplicity of form, sophisticated choice of material and color, with sections usually rounded, refined tenon joints, delicate moldings, and reduced, accentuated ornamentation. After the Ming dynasty, especially during the later years of the Qing dynasty, an overelaborated style of architecture appeared along with other art forms of that period. Succinct beauty and rustic charm seemed to be out of place. The Qing dynasty style of furniture tends to be bulky in sections, dark in color, and heavily decorated, sometimes with inlaid mother-of-pearl. Loaded down with trivial details, the overelaborate Qing dynasty furniture (fig. 7.43a, b, c) can be easily distinguished from the Ming dynasty's style of classic elegance (fig. 7.56).

Pavement (fig. 7.57)

Pavement is another original form of handcrafted art in the Chinese garden. Materials and patterns varied greatly with locality, adding particular environmental appeal. Natural rocks are used for constructing steps on artificial hills. Irregular stone plates, pebbles, crushed stones, or bricks are used to pave paths or courtyards, creating a natural and rustic look (fig. 7.58). The ground of the open walking galleries is often paved with bricks in the form of simple geometric patterns, or with gray, square, terra-cotta floor tiles. Elegantly worked stone and finely polished, square, terra-cotta floor tiles are used for terraces in front of halls and boatlike houses; they lend a sense of continuity with the indoor flooring. Waste material available in the construction field is composed into fascinating floor patterns. Pebbles, crushed stones, pieces of brick, curved roof tiles, broken porcelain or earthenware — with variety of color and texture — were used to make geometric patterns and realistic pictures of plant and animal life (figs. 7.59a to f). Compared to the colorful and elaborate Islamic mosaic floor, the pavement in the Chinese garden has a distinctive rustic touch in harmony with subtleness and elegance.

CHAPTER EIGHT
Plant Material

Plants are manipulated with special attention and methodology that contribute to the Chinese garden's unique style. With the extraordinary number of buildings and rockeries within the garden, there are relatively fewer plants than in gardens of other traditions. Plants do, however, retain importance as a unifying garden element that blends the artifacts with their surroundings, creating a naturalistic landscape.

Plants are carefully selected and applied as the center of interest; they serve as components of a scenic composition or as a foil in garden scenes. Buildings are often named after the plants cultivated around them; examples are the Magnolia Hall, the Pines and Breezes Pavilion, and the walking gallery called Willow-Shaded Winding Path in the Unsuccessful Politician's Garden.

The function of planting as a structural component for space disposition or as a partitioning device, as found in occidental gardens, is extensively taken over by walls because land is limited. Therefore, plants with open foliage are ranked over bulky shrubs or hedges with dense foliage. Trees are planted in small numbers; three to five trees strategically located can represent a grove in the pictorial composition. Bosquet and copse are cultivated for space division in large gardens only. Shrubs are often planted on hills of larger scale to serve as foils. Trees are especially favored in smaller areas and are said to be "occupying the sky but not the land," as the trunk takes little space and the crown spreads above human height (fig. 8.1). The deciduous Chinese parasol tree is the favorite within small areas. Its umbrellalike crown provides a cooling sunshade in summer, and the cheerful sunshine penetrates the bare twigs in winter. Fascinating shadows cast as patterns on pavements and walls are remi-

niscent of charming Chinese brush paintings. Shade trees with crowns floating above the sky also serve as horizontal shelters, and their outreaching branches act as transitions joining the enclosed space in buildings to the unbuilt, open spaces of courtyards and watercourses.

The bark of trees is also taken into consideration, especially in small courtyards and places of chance human contact. The Chinese parasol tree is an especially good courtyard planting because of its smooth and clean bark of a lovely light-green color (fig. 8.2). Its large leaves are easy to collect for disposal during the leaf-shedding season or can be temporarily left on the ground to be appreciated, as expressed in many traditional poems.

Plants in scenic compositions, when intended for close-up viewing, are not chosen merely for their posture. The detailed elegance of branches, the texture of leaves, the color, and the fragrance are all taken into careful consideration. Antiquity, distinctiveness, and gracefulness are the criteria for plant selection.

Slow-growing trees with artistically twisted and turned stems and branches, such as the crepe myrtle, the redbud, and the locust are favored for confined

FIG. 8.2 *The Chinese parasol tree has a smooth, clean bark that is especially suitable for garden locations subject to constant human contact; in Yu Yuan, the Pleasing garden, Shanghai.*

locations (fig. 8.3). Wisteria and other species of vine are planted to half-screen other garden components, to decrease the overpowering mass of a building, to soften the sight of a dazzling whitewashed wall, or to conceal an unsightly object such as an aesthetically weak connection between different garden components.

Bamboo groves are widely planted, in diverse quantities, around courtyards and buildings as an ideal screening and foiling device for their singular translucent effect (fig. 7.27). The unusual texture and jade-green color of the foliage contrasts beautifully with most of the other plants. In the larger courtyards and scenic sections, ginkgo and the southern magnolia are other favorite evergreen trees placed in positions that provide partial shade to courtyards and buildings. The nandina and the red dwarf maple are loved for their decorative leaves and brilliant scarlet colors, which highlight scenic compositions. Flowering plants contribute their special fragrances and blossoms. Among the low-rise scenic features of the Chinese garden, tall trees play important roles, leading the eye upward by drawing attention to their twigs and foliage in the sunlight, simulating a vertical visual expansion of space (figs. 8.4, 8.5).

Lawns are not completely absent from traditional gardens, as some observers have remarked, but they are usually planted in small areas. The beauty of the lawn in an occidental landscape garden is best perceived in large tracts of land with inexhaustible sight ranges. This contradicts the Chinese garden design principle of "avoiding total exposure of everything at a glance," and the stringent use of land in private gardens.

Different species of orchids, day lilies, lily turf, and ferns with graceful, drooping leaves are extensively planted in rock-and-plant composition as an unfailing transitional feature that integrates rocks to each other and to the ground (fig. 8.6).

The locality of plants is determined by topography, orientation, water supply, and other conditions necessary to their growth. The shade-tolerating camellia, nandina, osmanthus, boxwood, and privet are often attached to a wall or to the side of a building; the drought-tolerating pine, cypress, elm, and date trees are found on hills; the weeping willow and pomegranate, preferring moist soil, embellish watercourses. Nevertheless, considerations of better growth are not the only factors in plant arrangement. Plants are cultivated in relation to scenic compositions and must be well integrated into the entire garden entity.

When exotic plants are used, in certain cases an appropriate artificial microclimate is created to provide them with conditions for survival. The ever-occurring whitewashed wall, an excellent background for scenic composi-

FIG. 8.3 (opposite top) *A moon gate in the Unsuccessful Politician's Garden is adorned with rockery and trees of limited growth.*

FIG. 8.4 (opposite, bottom left) *Giant bamboos shade the pathway of a scenic mountain in southern China.*

FIG. 8.5 (opposite, bottom right) *A scenic view in Liu Yuan, the Lingering Garden, Suzhou, is greatly enhanced by the presence of soaring ancient pines.*

FIG. 8.6 (below) *A rockery enlivened with vines, lily turf, and drooping plants of limited growth; in the Surging-Wave Pavilion garden, Suzhou.*

tions, also serves as a wind shelter for plants (fig. 8.7). The beloved plantain trees are always positioned in small courts, beside a building or in another wind-sheltered corner, to ensure that their gigantic leaves are protected from being torn by the wind (fig. 8.8). Flowers and other delicate plants are protected from direct sunlight by being placed under trees or larger plants in a picturesque way.

Different species of plants and their pictorial compositions, common to garden scenes, are the favorite subjects of Chinese poetry and paintings. The symbolic significance of certain plants is chosen as emblems for blessings. Pomegranates and finger lemon, called "Buddha's hand" in Chinese, are planted for their spectacular fruits and also as auspicious symbols of prosperous offspring and longevity, respectively. The well-grown, symmetrical plants that occidental garden makers seek are too botanical and specimenlike to be compatible with Chinese taste, which prefers grotesque trees that add an air of dignity and antiquity to the garden.

Soaring pines and junipers sculptured by the hardship of time and weather —valued for their age and indomitable spirit, and as a symbol of longevity— are the ever sought-after models for cultivation. Pine trees are often cultivated with branches stretching out in one direction, reminding one of the "welcoming guest pine" in the scenic mountain Huang Shan (fig. 1.2). The beautifully clustered open foliage and magnificent silhouettes of these pines not only captivate the attention of beholders with their immediate form but are also intended to make the beholders imagine themselves visiting or revisiting the famed scenic mountain Huang Shan.

A variety of dwarfed plum trees with crooked, knuckled branches, blooming gorgeously during a severe winter snow, symbolizes an unconquerable spirit such as the struggle of humankind with hardship and survival. This symbolic indomitable spirit contrasts with the delicate or rather fragile-looking blossoms, further enhancing their attractiveness.

The chrysanthemum, endearingly described as the "late fragrance," is extensively cultivated as a symbol for "those who defy frost" and "those who survive all others." Physically, it contributes to the garden scene of late autumn with blossoms of innumerable shapes and colors. The lotus flower, captivating center of a summer scene, is adored as a symbol of purity and truth as it rises spotless from its bed of mud (figs. 7.6, 7.8). The opulent and colorful tree peony, having been referred to as the "king of flowers," is a symbol of wealth, nobility, and prosperity. It forms a contrast to the aromatic orchid's delicate charm. Orchids are loved for their subtle fragrance, blossoms of refined beauty, and especially their sheathlike leaves that suggest both strength and gracefulness.

Plants are thus personalized to present a certain mood, will, morality, or personality in a solitary display or group composition; these qualities are just as important as their functional and decorative sides. Therefore, the presence of plants in Chinese garden scenes not only affords aesthetic satisfaction but exhilarates the spirit and imbues viewers with the original intention of the garden maker.

FIG. 8.7 (left) *A grove of bamboo is planted on a lake rock parterre. The lily turf blends beautifully with the rock, both in color and texture; in the Pleasure Garden, Suzhou.*

FIG. 8.8 (below) *Plantain trees with spectacular leaves are planted in wind-sheltered garden spots.*

Terms used to describe group plant compositions enrich the Chinese garden vocabulary. Set combinations of plants, varied in design, are a special form of art consistent with Chinese painting. There are reasons for the constantly occurring combinations of plum blossom trees, orchids, bamboo, and chrysanthemum all famed as the "four virtuous gentlemen." They symbolize the praise of sincere friendship. The stretching, sculptured branches of the plum blossom tree, dark in color, contrast with the straight, smooth, shining jade-green stems of the bamboo. The chrysanthemum and the orchid fulfill the medium-height and ground-cover requirements, respectively, of a balanced scenic composition. Contrasting texture and color of leaves and flowers are also taken into consideration. With all these qualifications, the "four virtuous gentlemen" and many other popular plant combinations deserve to be beloved recurring garden scenes as well as the favorite subjects of traditional paintings.

Limiting the use of plants to native or naturalized species adaptable to regional climates is stressed in order to minimize maintenance work. Naturalized plants keep greater vitality and grow more rapidly into the intended posture of maturity to establish a well-balanced scenic composition.

The Chinese garden maker is clearly aware that the tendency to overload with different species of plants, as attractive or exotic as they may individually be, causes gardens to resemble one another. Restriction of planting, by emphasizing a particular plant or plants in a garden, intensifies the garden's individuality.

Weeping willows greatly enhance the charm of large watercourses such as the West Lake in Hangzhou and the Kunming Lake in the Summer Palace, Beijing. Willows planted along the banks and the causeways, alternatively with peach blossom trees, have become the special springtime scenic view of the West Lake (fig. 3.4) Willows were seldom cultivated along ponds of limited size in Suzhou gardens because the Suzhou native willow, with low, drooping, dense foliage, obstructs the sightline and impairs the spaciousness of water scenes in smaller gardens. A special kind of weeping willow in Yangzhou — endowed with a branching height unobstructive to human sightline and a translucent, veil-like foliage — is extensively cultivated and has become a special attraction of Yangzhou gardens. Mei Yuan, the Plum Garden, in Wuxi is known for the extensive cultivation of plum blossom trees.

The dimensions of architecture, artificial hills, watercourses, and the spaces consequently formed are consistent, but plants comprise the growing and changing factor of a garden. Uncontrolled plant growth often obliterates the original garden design. Therefore, plants of limited growth are favored for scenic compositions. Various methods, including trimming and root pruning, are used to suppress plant growth. It is against Chinese taste to clip shrubs into geometric forms. Trimming is practiced with sophisticated taste, only to improve the natural grace. Selected plants are trimmed to blend with their settings, such as adjoining buildings or other garden features, in the way they might naturally grow. Trees of grotesque and unusually balanced form found in scenic spots in mountainous areas, grown to survive under the hardship of the natural environment, have always been the admired models for trimming.

Thus, the unique aesthetic principles for the cultivation of plants in Chinese gardens do not exclude but allow occasional pruning while demanding that no trace of the practice be evident.

As nature is believed to be the source of manifold beauty, plants are given time to grow so that they naturally manifest their artistic forms. The aesthetic sense and imagination of the garden maker are, thus, to be inspired. Under such a conception and methodology, innumerable innovative garden scenes were created. This unique way of applying and manipulating plant life greatly reduces the need for maintenance work, which is an exceptional merit of the Chinese garden.

CHAPTER NINE
Literature and Art

A unique characteristic of the Chinese garden is its close association with the art and literary realms, and the integration of poetry, painting, and garden is the culmination of Chinese garden art. The Chinese traditional garden is governed by the rules of a theory of artistic creation that evolved hand in hand with other forms of Chinese culture, especially traditional painting. It was directly influenced by trends in contemporary painting of different eras in history and various schools of art.

Many antique landscape paintings attained eminence by depicting garden scenes. Successful scenes, in their turn, were constructed with famous paintings as models. The theme or tone of a garden might also depict the enchantment of a poem. Many garden scenes visualized selected verses from popular poems by famous poets; thus, the Chinese garden is also celebrated as "embodied poetry." In fact, Chinese gardens were designed to be "read" like romantic novels, like well-constructed essays in their fully developed literary form. The garden touring routes, to be discussed in Chapter Ten, organize Chinese gardens into sequential compositions. Invitational prelude, exciting climax, thought-provoking postlude—and numerous interludes as transitions for elaboration in scenic zoning and design—are beautifully practiced in the Unsuccessful Politician's Garden (plan 1.A), the Lingering Garden, and other large gardens. This fascinating characteristic of Chinese garden art could only have been originated and nurtured in a country with an exceedingly long history and profound cultural achievements.

Since Chinese gardens were designed with dominating themes to express particular emotions, and even scenic spots might be dedicated to a certain

concept, every garden has tablets or plaques bearing inscriptions of titles or verses composed during certain historical periods by eminent people of letters. The inscriptions use poetic wording and beautiful calligraphy to lend artistic enjoyment as well as literary satisfaction. Tablets and plaques were set up to elicit visitors' poetic responses as well as to stimulate visual pleasure.

Every garden (figs. 9.1, 9.2), each building (figs. 9.3, 9.4), and even some individual garden scenes (figs. 9.4, 9.5) invariably had a beguiling name expressing literary allusions. The name Lingering Garden depicts the garden as being so captivating that visitors would be reluctant to leave. The Net Master's Garden, meaning the Fisherman's Garden, implies the owner's love for the water and his admiration for the simple life led by fishermen. Thus, the water scene is intentionally the center of interest in this garden, with the best views arranged around a central pond (plan 2). The Unsuccessful Politician's Garden was built by a dismissed Ming dynasty courtier. He titled his garden Zhuozheng Yuan, which could also be interpreted as Stupid Administrator's Garden, to express frustration for his unsuccessful experience in the imperial court. Because a prominent scholar in Chinese history is addressing himself as stupid, the garden is also interpreted as the Humble Administrator's Garden.

Wooden plaques in horizontal form — elaborately painted and inscribed — are hung over gateways, on the back walls of halls (fig. 7.46b) or pavilions, often flanked by vertical panels inscribed with antithetical couplets or verses with matching designs. The plaque often indicates the title of the particular scenic spot, or points out the building's purpose or conceptual idea or the beauty of the views surrounding it. Panels are inscribed with verses that further describe the view or suggest philosophical thoughts provoked by the garden scene (fig. 9.2). These are very often ambiguous, allowing beholders the liberty of interpreting in their own way. Plaques or panels laquered in black, with golden inscriptions or gilded background with black lettering, are usually found in more formal settings, while polished natural wood or bamboo plaques and panels with brilliant green lettering are intended for a more casual and subtle look. Thus, even the color of these singular features is planned to highlight the scenes and enhance the planned emotional appeal.

Inscribed rocks in their natural shapes are mainly for outdoor use (fig. 9.6). The inscriptions are in color, preferably green, black, or vermilion, to highlight garden scenes. The lettering can also be left unpainted, to be examined at a close range, when it is intended to be a surprise discovery. Ashlar stone tablets were generally used only for the inscriptions of emperors, commemorating their visits. Pavilions were built to protect as well as to accentuate these tablets. Tablets inscribed with the remarks, comments, and calligraphy of Emperor Qianlong are incorporated in the Lion Grove, the Surging-Wave Pavilion, the Summer Palace, and many other scenic spots (fig. 9.7).

Black slate or stone tablets (fig. 9.8) are found inlaid in walls along open galleries and other types of buildings (fig. 9.9). These engraved or inscribed verses not only recorded the garden's history (fig. 9.10), or the writer's appreciation of its physical beauty, but also expose the feelings or moods he had

FIG. 9.1 (opposite, top left) *The entry of Jixiao Shanzhuang, the Roar-Resounding Mountain Villa, Yangzhou.*

FIG. 9.2 (opposite, bottom) *The entry of Ou Yuan, the Lotus Roots Garden, Suzhou.*

FIG. 9.3 (opposite, top right) *The Jade Green Light Pavilion in Qiuxia Pu, the Autumn Clouds Garden, Shanghai. Paintings and poems written in artistic calligraphy are mounted on the removable wall panel partitions.*

FIG. 9.4 *The tablet is inscribed with the title of the walking gallery, the Willow-Shaded Winding Path, in the Unsuccessful Politician's Garden, Suzhou.*

FIG. 9.5 *A rockery plant scenic composition in the court of the Spring Home of Begonia, the Unsuccessful Politician's Garden.*

FIG. 9.6 *A scenic view in Yi Yuan, Suzhou, with a rock inscribed with the title of the scene.*

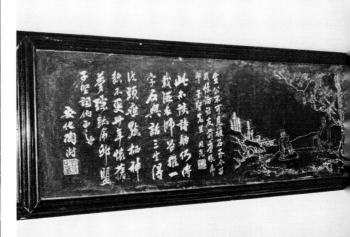

FIG. 9.7 (top left)   *A tablet in the Surging-Wave Pavilion garden, Suzhou, inscribed with the calligraphy of a Qing dynasty emperor.*

FIG. 9.8 (top right)   *Black slates inscribed with line-drawing paintings and verses written in beautiful calligraphy; they are important as a reference collection for calligraphy students.*

FIG. 9.9 (bottom left)   *Xin'an Garden for Tablets, Xi Xian, Anhui Province. Black stone slates inscribed with works of famous poets and calligraphers are inlaid on walls of halls and galleries.*

FIG. 9.10 (bottom right)   *The history of the Surging-Wave Pavilion garden, Suzhou, is written in elegant calligraphy of di style mounted on wall panels.*

been moved to express on viewing the garden. In fact, these tablets and couplets, interpreting the "painter's eyes and the poet's feelings," serve as guides to the gardens and have most effectively inspired later visitors with the delectation the artists had experienced. Although some of the verses were proverbs or thought-provoking personal remarks unrelated to the garden scenes, they contributed to the gardens' cultural interest. Thus, the Chinese closely integrate various forms of art and use the interaction of ancient artists to satisfy the visitor's quest for more than simple visual enjoyment.

Paintings were indispensable as decorative wall hangings (fig. 6.11); they were also mounted on partition panels (fig. 9.3). The evolution of garden styles in different regions was guided by the style of original landscape paintings and even of particular periods in history. For instance, the gardens in Yangzhou are distinctly different in character from those of Suzhou. These differences seem due not only to the different functional needs or garden materials used but also to the different schools of painting and styles of literature developed in these ancient cities. The Yangzhou gardens are bold and lively, influenced by the landscape paintings of the famous "eight queer painters" who had formed an outstanding school of art in Yangzhou. The style of poetry and literature, as well as painting, in Yangzhou was exuberant and ebullient, while the Suzhou schools of art were dainty and subtle. Garden styles developed correspondingly in these cities.

Ancient gardens were the favorite subject of ancient Chinese literature. They formed a common background in classic fiction, and there were not many theoretical garden books other than *Yuan Ye* of the Ming dynasty. Many scenes in the famous gardens were created according to these fictional and poetic descriptions. *A Dream of the Red Chamber* probably contains the most detailed account of a garden in the history of fiction. It is amazing that the Daguan Yuan, the Grand View Garden, which is the background of the major events in *A Dream of the Red Chamber,* was brought to life in a model constructed according to the fictional description. Actual gardens were built to recreate inner gardens of the Grand View Garden, as described in the book. One was Yihong Yuan, the Happy Red Court, in a Shanghai suburb. Amazingly and most amusingly both the model and the actual garden are recognizable to beholders who are familiar with the book. Thus, the Chinese garden is intimately related to all forms of Chinese culture in a way that is not found in any other garden in the world.

PART THREE

Design Process and Essence

CHAPTER TEN

Design Process

Site and Concept

Site investigation and exploration of natural landscape resources are given major emphasis in the ancient Chinese garden-building manual *Yuan Ye.* It asserts that the most important problem of garden design is how to conform with the shape and natural configuration of the site. It further suggests that in physical design planners must seek inspiration from the site's characteristic environmental atmosphere. That is, they must generate a novel design concept for a proposed garden based on the actual context of the site. Thus, capturing the characteristics of a site — improving it while attempting to retain its natural charm — and exploring the neighboring landscape resources to integrate them into garden scenes are two crucial approaches in creating an original garden. To follow nature's inherent laws and make the utmost use of them is a fundamental Chinese garden design principle.

The northwest suburb of Beijing contains most of the famous northern gardens, including the Summer Palace and the once glorious garden Yuanming Yuan, the Garden of Perfect Brightness. The sites were chosen because of the beautiful mountain ranges, West Hill and Jade Fountain Hill, which serve as magnificent backgrounds for the gardens (plan 14.C). Easy access to the city of Beijing was another important factor in site selection. Abundant water resources were directed from the mountains to form the water scenes in the gardens, including the magnificent artificial lake, Kunming Hu, of the Summer Palace (plan 14.A) and the innumerable lakes and canals that once flourished in Yuanming Yuan (plan 16).

Yuan Ye advises against imposing any conceivable order upon the beauty of

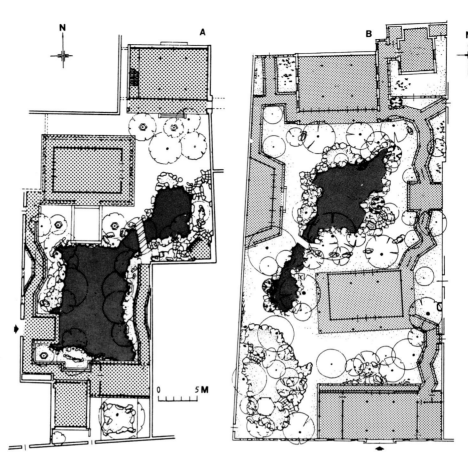

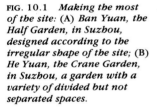

FIG. 10.1 *Making the most of the site: (A)* Ban Yuan, *the Half Garden, in Suzhou, designed according to the irregular shape of the site; (B)* He Yuan, *the Crane Garden, in Suzhou, a garden with a variety of divided but not separated spaces.*

FIG. 10.2 *The Spring and Autumn Tower, Chunqiu Ko, in Li Yuan, the Seashell Dipper Garden, Wuxi — providing lake views of scenic Tai Hu from different levels — is criticized for being overpowering in scale.*

the natural landscape; it suggests, rather, endeavoring to make constructed features fit into the natural contexts with the ultimate purpose of creating beautiful, original gardens.

In site selection, wooded hills, chosen for their secluded beauty that suggests the wilderness, are given priority in *Yuan Ye*. Scenic spots on lofty mountains, wherever a supply of fresh water exists, have been the sites of Buddhist or Taoist monasteries and temples since time immemorial. As cultivated artists with refined taste, the ancient monks and priests were able to convert these mountainous areas into livable environments and successfully highlighted the natural mountain charms by crowning them with artifacts.

A vast body of placid water veiled in mist was recommended in *Yuan Ye* as another excellent setting for a garden. Changing clouds in the background, floating fishing boats in the distance, and water birds wandering along the shore could all be included as endowments of the site.

The countryside and suburbs are favored in *Yuan Ye* over populous and busy city sites for gardens. Ancient garden owners, however, reluctant to forsake the convenience of city life, and trying at the same time to retain the enjoyment of natural landscape without the trouble of traveling, promoted the creation of the most successful gardens within the cities of Suzhou and Yangzhou, for example. Thus, fabulous artificial landscapes were created through human effort upon pieces of plain land within unfavorable contexts of limited area. Creating naturalistic landscapes in city areas was proved not only practicable but successful.

Pieces of land attached to the back or sides of residences, had been converted to fascinating gardens regardless of size and shape (fig. 10.1). Through the construction of myriads of private gardens, with the Suzhou gardens as the archetype, garden design principles were crystallized; but the application of these principles was very versatile. Ancient Chinese garden masters accumulated an abundance of experience with mature design techniques, developed a unique vocabulary of garden architecture through thousands of years of practice, and thus created the glorious history of Chinese garden art. The Suzhou garden beautifully illustrates possibilities and ways of establishing a fascinating, viewable, tourable, and livable environment on an uninteresting plot within ordinary city blocks.

The task of garden design includes commanding and promoting the enjoyment of existing landscape. Hence, it is wise to build garden views that complement rather than compete with the natural landscape. A three-story building, Chunqiu Ge, the Spring and Autumn Tower, was erected in Li Yuan, the Seashell Dipper Garden, in Wuxi, to command the best view of the lake Tai Hu through viewing points at different levels (fig. 10.2). Unfortunately, this building is considered too conspicuous, with its overly glamorous architectural design and overpowering scale; it is in competition with the beauty of the natural lake.

Chinese traditional gardens were supposed to be well-balanced ecosystems requiring little maintenance. Thus, water was seldom introduced artificially. Water supply was taken into consideration first in site selection. The city of Suzhou, with an abundance of water resources and a high underground water table is known as a "village of water." Many of the famous Suzhou gardens were built on marshlands of little use or value. Lakes were formed by excavation to give proper depth to the water bed. Earth raised to form hills or islands of various shapes served to complicate the ground form, enriching and beautifying the garden views.

The construction of buildings and the formation of hills and water could be accomplished in a reasonable time, but it took generations to witness the growth and development of trees into artistically sculptured shapes. Aged trees existing on the site were valued for their conspicuous contribution to the exquisite air of dignity and antiquity sought in the Chinese garden (fig. 8.5). There was great effort to preserve and organize existing trees into garden views; as a result, they often became beloved specialties of the gardens. Thus, Chinese gardens, as romantic as their aesthetic presentations may be, are rational in design right from their schematic concept.

According to the design principle of "follow the site to create the best," a careful study of the site's physical context was demanded to create an emotional appeal in the scenic sights. This was an extremely challenging task, but great success was often obtained by winning trying battles in the design field.

General Layout
(fig. 10.3)

The garden's general layout depends on the physical context of the site (its size and topography), the functional needs of the garden, the neighboring landscape resources, and the visual and emotional atmosphere the garden maker wishes to create.

Traditional private gardens were often adjacent to the formal residence, at the rear or the side of a courtyard house. They were built for the pursuit of a romantic lifestyle, as opposed to being confined by architectural restrictions of the formal residence; hardly any effort of integrating the garden with the adjoining formal courtyard house can be found. Connections were made with doors wherever convenient (fig. 10.3), and gardens usually had separate access to the street.

A typical private garden layout is shown in fig. 10.4. A screening feature is often found at the entry, with a set of elegant rockery or a display of graceful whitewashed wall as the favored themes. A sizable hall is indispensable, sitting across a pond, opposite the central garden scene; most often, there is also an artificial hill reflected in a pond. Pavilions, galleries, and other garden features may be allocated to the banks of the central pond or perched on the hill as complementary scenes. Bridges and footpaths link the diverse water scenes and "mountain views."

In order to fulfill the requirements of a living environment while suggesting a vast naturalistic landscape in a limited space, gardens were divided into sections for varied functional needs and scenic disposition. This demanded a superb cultivation of artistic and technical skill.

The Chinese garden developed into a unique composition of irregular, asymmetric, curved, crooked, undulating lines, planes, and forms derived

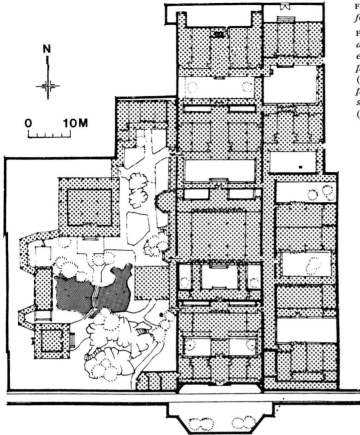

FIG. 10.3 (top) *A garden attached to a formal courtyard house in Suzhou.*

FIG. 10.4 (bottom) *Basic components and layout of the Chinese garden:* (A) *entry;* (B) *main hall;* (C) *terrace;* (D) *pond;* (E) *artificial hill;* (F) *courtyard;* (G) *rockery;* (H) *walking gallery;* (J) *pavilion;* (K) *water pavilion;* (L) *streamlet;* (M) *pathway;* (N) *bridge;* (O) *plants;* (P) *wall.*

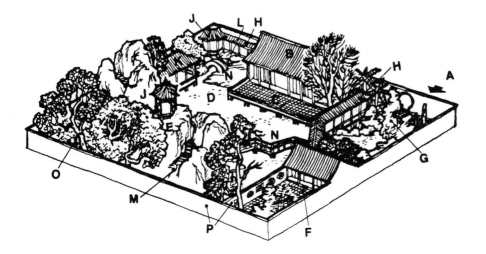

from nature; it generally, not absolutely, avoided straight lines, paths, and artificial order of any kind, ultimately creating a built environment with architectural and natural elements composed into a wonderfully integrated entity.

An exceptional example is the garden at the rear of the Imperial Garden, Beijing. It is a most peculiar Chinese garden with relatively generous land use: The entire garden was planned with strictly axial, symmetrical layout. This garden is recognized as being authentically Chinese only because of its more typical Chinese garden features.

Symmetrically designed court gardens are found in temples, monasteries, palaces, and on the main axis of a formal residence in a relatively small area. Each courtyard garden is embellished with special garden features—such as plants, watercourses in the form of ponds or creeks, and even bridges—arranged to intensify the intended atmosphere of the specific architecture. Nevertheless, these courtyards cannot be recognized as real "gardens"; they consist of landscaping used as a foil to architecture in the contemporary conception of landscaping (fig. 10.5). Small courtyards in the formal residential courtyard houses are often embellished with scenic display of garden features, but they merely function as enlarged *bonzai*.

Despite the strong tendencies toward informal liveliness and asymmetric layout of the entire garden, the main hall generally retains the symmetrical architectural design and furniture arrangement that accommodate the needs for occasional formal social or family activities. The interior of the main hall in the garden closely resembles the hall in a formal courtyard house, except for the more fanciful carvings of its fenestration and other architectural details. This sizable building fits into the naturalistic, asymmetric planning of the garden by means of its succinct and unpretentious outward appearance, in contrast to other types of garden architecture that mostly have a tendency toward elaboration of form (fig. 7.6).

In the Summer Palace (plan 14.A), the former imperial courts and residences, incorporated in the garden, are all symmetrically designed to cope with the ritualistic demands of imperial life; these are Renshou Dian, Benevolence, Longevity Hall, Yulan Tang, Jade-Ripple Hall, Leshou Tang Happiness-Longevity Hall, and even the predominating architectural cluster of Fuxiang Ge, Buddhist-Fragrance Tower. These large extensions of axially laid out, symmetrically designed building complexes blend into a naturalistic landscaped environment through a plan of enclosed courtyards linked by transitional plants, rocks, and hills. An important point to note is that architecture takes the form of clusters instead of a massive single building and the larger halls are generally flanked or surrounded by smaller buildings or open pavilions that serve as transitions to the landscape settings. The presence of the lake, Kunming Hu, is the most effective unifying element of the entire garden (plan 14.A). The axial layout can be perceived only through an aerial view from the hilltops. Therefore, the garden's asymmetrical entity is not forfeited by the presence of divisional garden sections that have a rigidly symmetrical design.

Prior to designing a Chinese garden, the garden maker must consider two methods of viewing: static viewing and mobile viewing. The first calls for

FIG. 10.5 *A courtyard in a temple in symmetrical layout, Hangzhou.*

viewing points, as well as scenic spots, for lingering observation. Mobile viewing demands varied scenes organized in well-conceived sequences along a touring route or routes. If scenic spots for static viewing are to be assimilated as three-dimensional paintings, mobile viewing creates a four-dimensional picture of the garden by impressing beholders with continually changing views as they take their time strolling along touring routes. In a small-scale garden or within a scenic section, static viewing should predominate, with mobile viewing as the usual complement. In a large-scale garden, the points of interest for static viewing are organized to bring forth the magnificence of a mobile-viewing effect.

In conclusion, the zoning of scenic sections, the arrangement of scenic spots and viewing points, and the planning of touring routes are the major processes of Chinese garden design.

Space disposition and scenic sections   To create an enchanting constructed, thematic environment reproducing the various charms of nature within a limited area requires planning of space disposition and scenic sections as the preliminary steps. The more famous traditional gardens, ranging in area from half a hectare, the Net Master's Garden (plan 2), to 290 hectares, the Summer Palace (plan 14-A), were invariably subdivided into sections intimately interlocked with each other as integrated garden entities. Division into scenic sections is the fundamental measure taken to create seeming spaciousness in restricted areas. Subdividing the garden into more or less defined sections also provides the greatest liberty in arranging scenic views that are surprisingly different and have varied atmospheric expression. Viewers are exposed to special experiences that impress them with the illusion of having toured through a vast space. Therefore, garden scenes are concealed in scenic sections, to be disclosed not all at once but gradually in well-conceived sequences.

Among all the space-dividing devices used in Chinese gardens, walls and walking galleries rank first over other garden components (fig. 10.6). The wall occupies the least space, and the gallery is visually the least obstructive. The majority of large scenic sections are not completely partitioned. Artificial hills of varied sizes and design are used as a more natural and ornamental feature for confining scenic sections wherever ambiguous divisions are preferred. The configuration of undulating artificial-hill ranges and the formation of an open pond or a confined creek are the main factors of space disposition, creating divided and yet unified scenic sections of the Chinese garden.

Yuanming Yuan, Beijing, was praised as the "garden of thousands of gardens" for its numerous fascinating scenic sections (plan 16). It employs the above-mentioned method, with watercourses as the unifying media, and even has exotic baroque-influenced architecture laid out by a Jesuit Father Benoit under the emperor's commission. Being confined as sectional scenes, the architecture did not appear discordant in the Chinese garden context. Thus, when unusual elements appear as sectional scenes, major conflict with the garden entity is avoided.

In planning scenic sections, it is very important to accentuate the dominating part by giving it a larger space and a prominent garden scene. Generally, the main section is centrally located, surrounded by subordinate sections of various sizes. Every scenic section is endowed with its own characteristic theme, featuring various garden aspects.

The garden consists of spaces that include contrast: large versus small, open versus closed, elevated versus lowered, bright versus shaded. Contrast is a very essential approach in garden design that seeks to achieve a psychological effect that dramatically intensifies the artistic presentation and inspires the viewer's curiosity for further discovery. This is how the ancient Chinese garden maker managed to create captivating gardens.

The hill-and-water composition, requiring a large space, is invariably constructed as the focal point of the dominating section, which is often the central theme of the entire garden. Subordinating sections, relatively smaller in space and less conspicuously located, are often adorned with scenic views of greater variety in composition and with differing garden features (plan 1.A). These scenes are planned to be compatible with the art of Chinese painting in three-dimensional composition (fig. 10.7). Subordinate scenic sections can have the following forms: secluded courtyard; water scene, such as water court, rock-lined pools, winding streamlet, and waterfall; rockery of varying size and arrangement; plants of artistic posture; and pictorial compositions of these features contrasted with exquisite architecture of differing types, sizes, and heights together with artistically shaped walls.

Planning the space into individual sections satisfies various functional needs of the garden and also increases viewing pleasure. The dominating

FIG. 10.6 (top) *A wall with a moon gate and a crooked walking gallery divide the garden into scenic sections; in the Lion Grove garden, Suzhou.*

FIG. 10.7 (bottom) *Rockery scene in a court in the Net Master's Garden, Suzhou, is a "three-dimensional painting" framed with an elaborately carved wooden screen of the Cloud Ladder Chamber.*

section is usually the place for diversified living activities and large gatherings, such as parties, entertainment of friends, and family get-togethers. The sizable main hall, *tīng* or *tang,* is a basic building accommodation. Even a stage can be found, erected for Chinese opera or muscial performances.

The inner garden—or a secluded courtyard in a remote spot—affords an undisturbed environment for a den, guest house, or bedchamber. A wooded hill, a valley with a stream, a mysterious cave, or a grotto in the secluded area are places for further pursuing the enchantment of the wilderness.

With the above-mentioned strikingly different scenes providing divergent atmosphere, arranged in adjacent scenic sections, door openings of various shapes and window openings, with or without trellises, are provided on the walls for the purpose of *lou-jing*, which means divulged views — that is, to avoid abrupt changes by allowing a glimpse of the scenery concealed in one scenic section (figs. 10.8, 10.9). Divulged views also arouse the beholder's curiosity for continuing the garden tour into individual scenic sections.

The charms of a small scenic section could also be greatly enhanced by a "borrowed view," borrowing space from adjoining, larger scenic sections. A small scenic section can hardly afford to allow divulged views, however, without losing its attraction through the total exposure of major scenic views. "Divulging" and "borrowing" views are important transitional measures that seek to connect and to maintain harmonious unity between scenic sections of Chinese gardens.

Scenic spots and viewing points It is true in Chinese gardens that the "gardens excel with scenes and scenes vary with gardens," as demanded in creative designing. The originality and individuality of garden scenes add up to the success of a celebrated garden. Every garden scene should have its own point of interest — picturesque as a painting and lyrical as a piece of poetry — but the garden as a whole is unified under a central theme.

A pond of placid water, contrasted with magnificently molded rock hills, surrounded by complementary scenic features, and highlighted with different types of architecture is the typical layout of the central scene — with variations — in most Chinese gardens. The Unsuccessful Politician's Garden is a magnificent example of the larger garden; the Net Master's Garden exemplifies the smaller (plans 1, 2). The Grace-Surrounding Mountain Villa (plan 7) and the Surging-Wave Pavilion (plan 5) are rare examples of gardens dominated by a range of artificial hills. The former is supplemented by a meandering stream along the valley of the hills, and the latter is enlivened by a small pool. The innovativeness and captivating quality of the prominent garden scene greatly contribute to the success of these celebrated gardens.

The sizable main hall, *tīng* or *tang,* in the private gardens — such as the Distant Fragrance Hall in the Unsuccessful Politician's Garden (plan 1) and the dominating architectural cluster of Buddhist Fragrance Tower and Cloud-Dispelling Hall in the Summer Palace (plan 14.A) — is a place intended for major activities and gatherings. The best views of predominating garden scenes are provided there. Subordinate garden scenes are arranged around the central watercourse or perched on a dominating hill within sight of the Distant Fragrance Hall and the Buddhist Fragrance Tower.

These scenic-spots, in their turn, serve as viewing points for enjoying picturesque views, from different directions, of the Distant Fragrance Hall and the Buddhist Fragrance Tower on Longevity Hill. A garden view when exquisitely positioned to be seen from different directions presents changed views (figs. 10.10, 10.11*a, b*). Variety not only emphasizes the different aspects of a

FIG. 10.8 *From a courtyard in the Garden for Retreat and Meditation, a rockery in composition with a tree is viewed as a vista through an octagonal gate.*

FIG. 10.9 *View from the inner garden of the Unsuccessful Politician's Garden, Suzhou, through the moon gate, Leading to a New World.*

FIG. 10.10 (top)   *One garden scene viewed from different perspectives, presenting varied views.*

FIG. 10.11 (bottom)   *The teahouse in Guyi Yuan, Shanghai, the Ancient Magnificent Garden, viewed from different angles.*

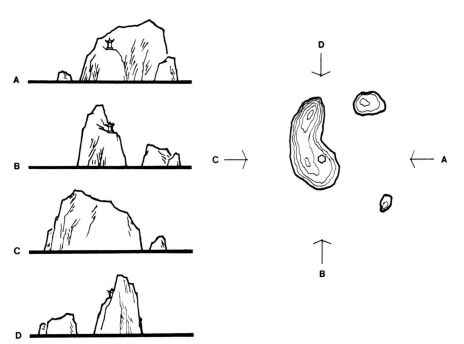

garden scene but also shows its changing backgrounds, which consist of the garden features seen around it. Repeated appearance of the same subject presented in different aspects and in varied sequences is also a visually unifying approach that effectively enhances a garden's harmonious beauty.

In Chinese gardens, natural landscape scenes and architectural features alternate in another sort of refreshing contrast. Natural landscape scenes composed of hills, water, rocks, and plants are created in a refined manner with seemingly natural forms. Single or grouped plants are cultivated as central scenes of the smaller scenic sections. Most often, scenic composition is modeled after traditional Chinese painting.

The Chinese garden includes an enormous quantity of architecture and yet is appraised as an authentic naturalistic garden. This fascinating success is attributed to the unobstructiveness of garden architecture in the form of open shelters, and the curved silhouette of floating roofs and pointed eaves is exquisitely merged into the curvilinear nature of landscape views.

Arrangement of the terminal scenes, the vistas, is important in sustaining the participant's interest. The sight line is not oriented on the axis as it is in western tradition, but it is focused from planned viewing points or led on along the paths and walking galleries by vistas arranged at turning points (fig. 10.12). The major terminal features of Chinese gardens are generally positioned at spots where the participant is likely to linger along the touring routes. Garden scenes are also subtly planned to be discovered as if by accident, fostering extra pleasure as surprises.

For the best viewing effect, the space between scenic spots and viewing points is carefully manipulated. In the Unsuccessful Politician's Garden, a body of water and a rather spacious terrace are introduced to provide a distance between the Distant Fragrance Hall and an isle with a span of artificial hill in the opposite direction (plan 1). Other garden scenes are dispersed around the central pond. The plantings of trees and flowers on the terrace serve as foils to the hall when the hall is viewed from different directions across the central pond and also serve as foreground when one is viewing from the hall. The water's reflection further beautifies the picturesque garden scenes along the pond.

In viewing individual scenic objects, it is important to keep the appropriate distance from objects of various size. For instance, because the height of artificial hills in Chinese gardens scarcely exceeds 7 meters, the viewing points are generally located at a distance of 12 to 35 meters in order to lend a taller image to the hills (fig. 7.4). As for the lower solitary display of rockery, less distance provides an illusion of loftiness that is gained through perspective (figs. 10.13, 10.14).

Location of scenic spots and viewing points is not arrived at merely by horizontal planning. Scenic spots for various garden features are carefully designed, with diversified heights and silhouettes, and are planned at varied elevations that follow the constructed or natural contours of the site (fig. 10.15). Vertical compositions complete the variety of the garden scenes and also afford the pleasure of viewing from vantage points at different levels. Elevated viewing points bring about more open and wider sight range over the tops of trees, artificial hills, and water courses, with a possible glimpse into a secluded wooded valley. The lower, ground-level water pavilion or bridge fosters a broader perspective of the water surface and a loftier impression of the surrounding artificial hills, buildings, and trees.

Scenic spots are designed for static viewing, that is, for lingering observation from well-planned viewing points in different directions, most often with the best façade facing toward the main viewing point (fig. 10.7). A den or studio occupying a dominating position in an enclosed courtyard oriented toward the south is opposed with an elegant scenic composition backed by a whitewashed wall as a "three-dimensional painting" (figs. 2.5, 9.5). Here, the scenic views may be designed for viewing from one direction, but they are apt to be observed for a long period of time. Therefore, not only the general aspects of the composition are important, but so are the specific details; texture and color of the leaves and flowers of the plants are thus stressed in designing. Planning for this kind of static viewing often attempts to suit the mood of contemplation that is most likely to settle over the occupant of a den or studio.

Each garden scene is a work of art, its various components subject to artistic treatment such as contrast, setoff, scale, layer, vista, and "borrowed scene." Thus, the Chinese garden fosters mobile viewing of dynamic beauty, and

FIG. 10.13 *The effect of loftiness is achieved by the relative positions of the viewing point and the objects viewed.*

FIG. 10.14 *A rockery in Ge Yuan, the Bamboo Leaves Garden, Yangzhou, set off by buildings in the background.*

FIG. 10.15 (top)   *Cross-section of the Unsuccessful Politician's Garden, Suzhou (plan 1.A): (22) Gate Hall, (21) Distant Fragrance Hall, (19) Leaning Jade Studio, (5) Leading to a New World, (18) Lotus Breezes from All Sides Pavilion, (23) Fragrant Snow and Azure Sky Pavilion, (10) Mountain View Mansion.*

FIG. 10.16 (bottom) *Redrawn from a traditional scroll painting.*

static views of diversified size and design, in varied locations, build up and highlight the garden's dynamic panorama.

Touring routes and vistas   Garden scenes — being analogous metaphorically to landscape paintings — are maintained in all naturalistic gardens, oriental and occidental; but the wonderful continuous composition of diversified spectacles can be found only in Chinese scroll paintings and gardens. The unique method of using perspective with mobile vanishing points and the concept of unlimited space continuity characterize scroll painting, which was a very popular form during the Yuan, Song, and Tang dynasties. These techniques greatly influenced the style and evolution of Chinese garden art.

Touring routes in the Chinese garden connect scenic spots and scenic sections in a well-conceived succession, giving the beholder a pictorial view

of extraordinary length that resembles a scroll painting. Wherever your glance lingers, you find a well-balanced composition (fig. 10.16). Moreover, the effect of mobile viewing in Chinese gardens—with viewing points moving along an exquisitely planned route—promotes time-space enjoyment far beyond paintings of any sort.

Thus, touring routes are essentially designed for the pleasure of mobile viewing. The Net Master's Garden is one of the best examples of a smaller garden, excelling in static views. Visitors also enjoy changing views when strolling from one spot to another around the central pond (fig. 10.17). This touring route is relatively short and planned in a simple way. The Unsuccessful Politician's Garden, one of the best larger private gardens, affords thrilling and ever-changing views along intricately planned touring routes. The rest stops along the touring routes offer static viewing of refined and focused scenes (plan 1, fig. 10.18).

FIG. 10.17 (top left)   *Viewing from the Water Pavilion for Washing Headgear String toward the Watching Pines and Appreciating Paintings Studio and the A Branch Beyond the Bamboo Studio across the central pond in the Net Master's Garden, Suzhou.*

FIG. 10.18 (top right)   *Viewing to the north with Green Ripple Pavilion as the end vista. The Dwelling Amidst Parasol Trees with four moon gates, on the right, is connected to the central islet by a crooked bridge. The North Hill Pavilion is built on the islet hidden in the groves; in the Unsuccessful Politician's Garden, Suzhou.*

FIG. 10.19 (center)   *San-tan-yin-yue, Three Pools for Moon Reflection, an island with ponds in the West Lake, Hangzhou, is characterized as "waters in the water." Elegant rockeries are positioned as vistas at the turnings of the crooked bridge built on the pond.*

FIG. 10.20 (bottom)   *A walking gallery attached to a wall and angled to form a tiny court that becomes a vista along the touring route. Stone bamboos are used for the court scene, which is illuminated by overhead daylight; in the Unsuccessful Politician's Garden, Suzhou.*

Chinese garden design could be perceived as the art of concealing and revealing. Diversified garden scenes are concealed through the zoning of scenic sections, while the touring routes serve to reveal the scenes in captivating sequence.

Crooked or curved paths, walking galleries, and bridges form touring routes that guide planning of the itinerary and direct the observer's sight line to garden scenes arranged as vistas in different directions (fig. 10.19). Vistas lead the visitor along the touring routes and denote changes in direction (fig. 10.12).

A well-planned system of touring routes unifies the garden (plan 1.B). Garden scenes within scenic sections are often partially revealed as vistas along touring routes. Garden scenes are also arranged as visual sidetracks to be viewed from a distance across ponds or courtyards, which attract viewers to further exploration (fig. 7.33). Thus, not only do the configured paths, galleries, and bridges lead the way along the touring route, but the disposition of vistas along the route or away from the route serves as a direct or indirect guiding device contributing to the success of the garden's touring itinerary. When visitors travel along the touring route and finally reach the spot observed from a distance, the pursued garden scene may be a drastic contrast to the previous one. The change is dramatically impressive but not abrupt, as previous observation of the scene from a distance has a psychologically unifying effect upon the beholder.

Emphasizing the predominant mode in order to distinguish it from the subordinate is another essential principle of Chinese traditional art. The planning of touring routes is no exception, with the main route guiding the viewer throughout the major scenic spots and also leading to supplementary touring routes for optional side trips.

Blatancy is avoided in the Chinese garden, especially in private gardens. Views are preferably arranged as unexpected discoveries or even allowed to be left undiscovered as an incentive for a second trip.

Generally, small-scale gardens have a single touring route. In the Net Master's Garden, for example, the dominating scenic section is concentrated around a pond (plan 2). The surrounding halls and pavilions open toward the pond and are connected by galleries forming the touring route, which rises and falls following the molded rocky shore. Entries to the exquisite inner garden in the west and the subtle secluded courtyard at the north were arranged along the route with *yin-jing,* introductory views (figs. 10.8, 10.9), that is, to provide glimpses of the inner garden or courtyard through wall openings. These fascinating framed views motivate the visitor to take a side trip to these secluded attractions.

A meandering, colonnaded walking gallery, attached to a wall, often turns away from the wall to be a partially detached, free-standing segment; it then turns back to the wall, forming a tiny court between the gallery and the wall for the arrangement of a miniature landscape scene (fig. 10.20). The scenery in the tiny court serves as a vista along the touring route, appearing attractive when approached from either direction along the gallery. It is even more picturesque when viewed from a direction perpendicular to the gallery, as its scenic features are then framed by the posts of the colonnaded gallery. With the contrasting whitewashed plastered wall as background, it strikingly resembles a traditional Chinese painting on rice paper. As the court is open overhead, it is relatively better lighted than the roofed gallery, as though an overhead spotlight is illuminating the scenery. Besides, the sudden change of lighting during a long walk intensifies the enchantment of this repeatedly applied garden feature, one practiced in varied compositions.

Serpentine paths and walking galleries are often connected by a zigzag bridge or by winding, hazardous stepping stones over watercourses. These are common ways of elongating the supplementary touring routes, as well as arranging viewing opportunities in different directions. Gloomy and mysterious tunnels undulating at different levels, enclosed in rocky artificial hills, are delightful as optional trips in larger gardens (fig. 10.21).

Touring routes undulate vertically in accordance with the rise and fall of the ground, allowing viewing from different heights (fig. 6.36). Different ranges of sightlines are provided. The visitor may travel up to the summit of an artificial hill for a far-reaching panoramic view (fig. 10.22) or down into the secluded serenity of a confined, wooded valley. Undulating walking galleries often romantically overhang the watercourse or are built on hills with slopes and steps to give the spectator changing viewing angles of elevation and depression (fig. 7.13). The flowing roof of the walking gallery synchronizes with its seemingly floating floor, displaying a graceful plasticity unusual in timber structures.

For further amusement, touring routes are designed to draw interest at different levels. The two-story walking gallery, one specialty of the Yangzhou garden, leads the touring route to elevated levels (fig. 6.13). Visitors mounting rocky hills greet fellow visitors who are passing beneath their footsteps through tunnels or gorges (fig. 10.23). It is equally delightful to linger on the arched bridges (figs. 6.29, 7.41) watching others boating through the arches. The abrupt change in viewing-point levels that occurs when visitors tour on a steeply arched bridge once again provides them with the pleasure of new viewing angles and sight ranges.

Open paths and covered walking galleries—undulating horizontally and vertically with infinite views unfolding along the way—are the favorite approach to planning a touring route, but this is not the only way in the Chinese garden. In the imperial gardens, with their large spans of land, including the Summer Palace and Beihai Park in Beijing, walking galleries serve as communicating devices between buildings. Since the scenic sections are also living quarters scattered in a vast territory, quick and efficient access to them is sensible. Therefore, straight pathways are not totally excluded. The colonnaded long galleries of the Summer Palace and Beihai Park are captivating and impressive because of their extraordinary distance span and their enormous number of structural bays (fig. 5.11). Picture frames formed by the columns of the galleries focus attention on water scenes of Kunming Hu and Beihai, and on other garden scenes. To further enrich the tourist's experience, the cross beams of each structural bay are adorned with painted, colorful pictures depicting various scenes of the gardens or even Chinese opera scenes. In this

FIG. 10.21 (top left) *Looking out from the grotto under the Summer Hill of Ge Yuan, the Bamboo Leaves Garden, Yangzhou. A single-plank crooked bridge leads from the grotto to paths that wind through rocky arches.*

FIG. 10.22 (top right) *A pavilion built on a rocky hill in an inner garden, Studio of Mental Peace, Beihai Park, Beijing, provides an elevated viewing point.*

FIG. 10.23 (bottom) *A plank stone bridge, crossing over a gorge in an artificial hill, forms the intersection of touring routes on different levels; in the Surging Wave Pavilion garden, Suzhou.*

way, the ancient Chinese garden maker took painstaking efforts to eliminate the monotony of a straight, linear path. These pictures also serve as an introductory catalog to the garden scenes.

This is an outstanding example of the ancient Chinese garden builder's inventiveness in solving a disadvantageous situation and converting it into a successful architectural feat. It was accomplished by following the Chinese garden design notion: "There are principles to be followed but no patterns to be copied." Creativity is, thus, highly demanded and ingeniously achieved.

CHAPTER ELEVEN

Creating Spaciousness in Limited Area

As most of the existing Chinese private gardens were built within ancient cities, limitation of land use was inevitable. On the other hand, to reproduce multifarious natural views requires a diversity of landscape features. To further complicate matters, a sophisticated living environment that accommodates daily functions and social needs involves a great quantity of buildings. All this tends to bring about cramped conditions in the garden. Nevertheless, the ancient Chinese garden makers successfully recreated the world of nature — not only in its beautiful form but with the spaciousness persistent in wild nature — within a drastically limited area. The ingenious methods underlying the successful gardens — creating vastness in a small area — are worthy of studying not only for garden design but as a valuable reference for architectural and landscape design.

Scale — A Key Point in Chinese Garden Design

Mastering scale is an essential design approach to creating seeming spaciousness in a limited area. Some observant participants refer to the Chinese garden as a "miniature landscape." Truly enough, the features of most private gardens are diminished in scale following the principle and methods of the *penjing,* the potted landscape, another unique form of Chinese-originated art (fig. 11.1).

The miniature potted landscape can be taken as an extreme in recreating natural landscape on a greatly diminished scale. Potted landscapes of differing size and scale are widely displayed in courtyards and as indoor, tabletop ornaments; they are praised as "mute poetry, three-dimensional painting, and living sculpture." In fact, this is a form of the smallest artificial landscape in the Chinese garden. Potted landscape migrated to Japan early in history and was well adopted, developing into its own style, which is known to the world as *bonzai.*

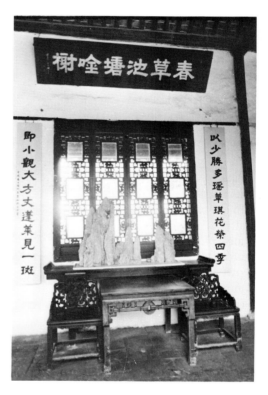

FIG. 11.1 (right)   *A potted landscape displayed in a water pavilion in the Slender West Lake, Yangzhou. A horizontal tablet is inscribed with the name of the place; the verses below it suggest the theoretical conception of the garden,* "less excels over more" *and* "seeing largeness through smallness."

FIG. 11.2 (bottom)   *Potted landscapes with different scales:* (a) *close-up view;* (b) *medium-distance view;* (c) *panoramic view.*

(a)   *(b)*   *(c)*

A general understanding of potted landscape helps to clarify methods of mastering scale in the Chinese garden. Potted landscapes executed in different scales depict views from diversified sight ranges, supposedly observed from varied distances. The key point of these accomplishments is the use of features in different scale. Three potted landscapes designed in different scale are shown for better comprehension: respectively, the close-up view, the medium-distance view, and the panoramic view.

In the close-up example (fig. 11.2a), stunted pines are cultivated, sometimes for hundreds of years. Root pruning and various ways of growth control are used to simulate the appearance of full-sized ancient and dignified pines. The presence of a few small stuccoed cranes successfully sets off an illusion that the pines are of a soaring height.

In the medium-distance example (fig. 11.2b), a pavilion and a winding footpath executed on an even smaller scale effectively suggest the loftiness of the miniature mountain. This gives the impression of a landscape much larger in size than the first example, though both are composed within a pot of the same size.

As for the third example (fig. 11.2c), a panorama of a mountain range is presented. No living animal figure or garden architecture of observable size would be appropriate to use for an extremely diminished scale. Stunted miniature pines, representing high mountain pines, are the scale that fosters incredible vastness in the composition.

The same principle and method are applied in the Chinese garden. Various scenic features are diminished in varied scale. Artificial hills and ponds are miniatures of natural mountains and lakes. Buildings of different types, especially those with two stories or those set upon artificial hills, are smaller in scale than normal. The miniaturization is judiciously carried out, so as to be scarcely noticed, but pleasantly introduces a sense of intimacy. Dwarfed or growth-controlled plants are the most effective for diminishing scale in scenic compositions. This is a way of presenting garden scenes with a seemingly larger size. It is fundamental to creating a feeling of spaciousness in the entire garden.

Consideration of scale must enter into the detailed design of garden views. Artificial hills intended for touring are molded to suit human scale. A footpath meandering along a pond into a valley between artificial hills is always designed in smaller but accessible width (figs. 2.7, 6.30, 6.36). Pathways are often paved with different materials so that they are not only decorative but also divided in width into smaller measurements that match the diminished size and scale of the surrounding garden features (figs. 11.3, 11.4).

Courtyard gardens and ponds within confined areas are furnished with smaller plants and rockeries, and other garden features proportioned to the dimensions of the space. Occasionally, certain plants are excluded from garden scenes because they are inappropriate in size despite being aesthetically pleasing. For instance, weeping willows are planted stooping over the water surface, with hanging branches rippling the spacious West Lake in Hangzhou (fig. 3.4) and other large bodies of water (fig. 11.5). In smaller private gardens with limited area, forsythia and other small drooping bushes are planted to

embellish ponds and rockeries; they replace the sizable weeping willows for a better scale. As for the rockery composition or rocky embankments of smaller pools in inner gardens, fern and lily turf are more suitable (fig. 2.5).

Bamboo may be one of the most widely cultivated plants in Chinese gardens. Many species of bamboo, with a great variety in size of leaves and stems, are available; their use greatly helps in creating scenic compositions of differing scale. Small-sized bamboo, with tiny spears, fits wonderfully in a potted landscape. Large-sized bamboo, with stems up to 6 inches in diameter and an enormous height, is commonly found as massive groves in natural scenic spots or around ancient monasteries (fig. 8.4). These vast areas are greatly enhanced by the proportional size of the soaring bamboos.

In constructing garden scenes merely for viewing purposes, great freedom is allowed in the use of small sizes that vary in scale in proportion to their background space. In fact, some of the inaccessible garden scenes are composed to resemble enlarged *bonzai* (figs. 2.5, 11.6).

Thus, all these techniques of mastering scale in the Chinese garden add to the simulation of spaciousness in a confined area, and they greatly contribute to the garden's intimate atmosphere.

Concealed Enclosure — Boundless Space

The walls enclosing private gardens or confining inner gardens tend to be concealed in some effective and attractive way. Walking galleries and other types of buildings are built to block the sight of boundary walls and to suggest

FIG. 11.3 (opposite, top left) *A winding path paved with different materials of varied size to form an attractive pattern; in the Summer Retreating Mountain Villa, Chengde.*

FIG. 11.4 (opposite, top right) *View south from a pavilion onto a pathway; notice the treatment of the pavement from a wider entry to a narrow footpath; in the Net Master's Garden, Suzhou.*

FIG. 11.5 (opposite, bottom) *The embankment of a pond in Bishu Shanzhuang, the Summer Retreating Mountain Villa, Chengde, enlivened by densely planted weeping willows.*

FIG. 11.6 (left) *A walking gallery and a half pavilion are attached to a two-story building to modify the building's overpowering effect on the scenic courtyard garden; Tingfeng Yuan, the Listen to the Maple Garden, Suzhou.*

a larger plot with more space behind the buildings (figs. 6.20, 11.7, 11.8). Plants are also extensively used for screening. Vines especially foster a touch of the charm of wilderness occupying minimal space. A rockery erected in front of a wall suggests that a generous space exists between it and the wall when they are viewed from a distance (fig. 11.9). A rockery in Ge Yuan partly attached to a wall is an original of space-saving form and is most appealing as a piece of art (fig. 11.10).

In a smaller garden site, buildings and sizable garden features are often arranged along the boundary walls. This kind of perimetric layout yields a relatively generous centralized space, enabling the inclusion of more garden features within the confined space. The Net Master's Garden stands as one of the best models (plan 2). Both its central garden and inner garden in the west follow the above-mentioned principle with great success but with different themes and details. In the main scenic section, elegant galleries, pavilions, and halls — set off by rockeries and plants — were planned more or less along the enclosure walls, leaving centralized space for a scenic pond. The mirroring effect of the placid water surface intensifies the spaciousness and the magnificence of the central garden (fig. 10.7), while the inner garden's paved terrace — a relatively generous area of its kind — is embraced by the subtly designed Late Spring Studio to the north, leaving a few feet further north for a tiny court with a miniatured landscape display. A gallery connected to the studio is attached to the east wall, a small range of rock hills adorns the south wall, and a half pavilion enlivens the west wall (fig. 11.11). Thus, the perimetric layout of the inner garden is completed. Both of these solutions contribute to the goal of serenity. In total area, the Net Master's Garden is only half a

FIG. 11.7 (bottom, left) *Different types of buildings attached to the boundary wall of Tingfeng Yuan, the Listen to the Maple Garden, Suzhou.*

FIG. 11.8 (bottom, right) *A half pavilion attached to a boundary wall in the Unsuccessful Politician's Garden, Suzhou.*

FIG. 11.9 (opposite, top) *The enclosure wall of Yu Yuan, Shanghai, partially concealed by elegant rockeries.*

FIG. 11.10 (opposite, bottom left) *A rockery attached to a building's end wall in Ge Yuan, the Isolated Garden, Yangzhou.*

FIG. 11.11 (opposite, bottom right) *The Late Spring Studio in an inner garden of the Net Master's Garden, Suzhou.*

hectare, and though its architectural density is as high as 30 percent, the garden still gives the illusion of remarkable spaciousness.

A neighboring eyesore not only impedes visual pleasure, it also reveals the area limits of a garden. Therefore, tall garden features, such as two-story buildings or rockeries, are set up for concealment; and when a towering distant view or a rockery behind a building is further organized into the garden view, the garden's space is seemingly multiplied in a dramatic way.

Curved, Crooked, and Undulating Layout

Curved, crooked, or vertically undulating paths plus bridges and walking galleries serve to define the touring routes of Chinese gardens and lead the beholder's attention toward views in different directions. Their freely curved lines and forms, imitative of nature, greatly contribute to the unity between artifacts and natural landscape features.

The curved, crooked, and undulating layout of Chinese gardens should not be taken merely as an expression of artistic creativity. It is another fundamental way of seeming to enlarge the dimensions of the garden. A narrow and serpentine footpath elongates the distance between two points, and it takes more time to cover an undulating path than a level, direct shortcut. Thus, this is a way of generating illusions, like some of the other techniques. It actually prolongs the distance and traveling time, but beholders never regret the extra distance they have to cover because they are rewarded with extra, fascinating viewing experiences.

Curved linear features such as paths and streams also help to foster a sense of spatial depth. Turnings divide the paths or streams into segments and thus effectively call up awareness of depth (figs. 11.12, 11.13), whereas it would take a considerable distance increase on a straight avenue to make the observer think it was longer, especially in the absence of any noticeable objects along the vista.

Most ponds in Chinese gardens are irregularly shaped. Promontories and inlets are constructed not only for ornamentation, to create a natural look, but to add effectively to the "depth" of the watercourse the way the turnings of a meandering pathway (fig. 11.14) add to its depth.

Another way of elongating touring paths and prolonging the duration of touring time is to use intersecting touring routes on different levels. A tunnel built through an artificial hill plus elevated paths upon the hill (fig. 11.15), an arched bridge with a boating route under it, an elevated walking gallery crossing over pathways are favorite design solutions. With the same area toured more than once, on different levels, the garden seems larger than actual size.

Divided, not Separated: Layers, Sequence, and Depth

The essence of spatial design observed in the Chinese garden is that space is "divided not separated." Divisions are formed to conceal or partly obscure scenic spots that will be discovered later, but there is always an opportunity to

FIG. 11.16 (top left) *A
perspective of the colonnade
of a walking gallery, seen
through a begonia-shaped
window opening in the
Slender West Lake Park,
Yangzhou, presents a scenic
view of infinite depth.*

FIG. 11.17 (top right) *A
walking gallery in Daguan
Lou, the Grand View
Mansion, a garden in
Kunming, Yunnan province,
is divided into sections with
walls pierced with flower-
vase-shaped door openings
that add greatly to the depth
of the gallery. The garden has
excellent water scenes that
include fascinating reflections
of the buildings on the placid
water surface.*

perceive a segment of the hidden view (fig. 11.16). Partial revelation of a
space encourages the viewer to imagine a space that is larger than its actual
size.

An undeveloped piece of land and an unfurnished room always look much
smaller before they are arranged with buildings or furniture. The objects
existing between the observer and a focal point help to mark the distances and
eventually seem to express depth through their cumulative effect (fig. 11.17).
A bridge spanning a pond, promontories and inlets, and drooping willows at
varied distances along the embankment both embellish and effectively add to
the depth of a watercourse. Smaller plants used as the foreground of viewing
points add greatly to the charms of layered water scenes (fig. 11.18). The
presence of isles, which can be merely symbolic piles of rocks (fig. 6.27) or
even plantings of water lilies (fig. 11.19), enhance the spaciousness of a
garden pond by marking the total area into sections.

Forms of buildings other than walking galleries (figs. 11.20, 11.21) are also
part of the garden's space structure. Buildings in the form of open shelters and
walls with fanciful windows or door openings mark distances but do not block
garden views and the continuity of garden space. An exquisite example is
found in Yu Yuan, Shanghai, where a partition wall crosses over a pond; its
fanciful crescent opening spans the water. The pond is thus divided, but the
viewer's sight flows with the water into the inner garden achieving a continual
space between different scenic sections (figs. 11.22, 11.23). With dividing
features and scenic views artistically arranged in sequential layers, an
enchanting illusion of mysterious depth is achieved (fig. 11.24). These

layered scenes are most important in creating the serenity of Chinese gardens.

Scenic sections can also be subdivided, for diversity of spatial presentation, by slightly changing the levels of land form or by using low partitions of plants and rocks (fig. 11.25). In this case, there is no risk of blocking the view.

The Studio of Mental Peace is celebrated as an outstanding example of spaciousness created in a small area by subdividing the space and providing diversified scenic views. The garden, with a limited lot of 7700 square meters, is divided into seven scenic sections of different sizes with varied scenes (plan 15.B). Buildings and artificial hills form the main divisional structure. Open galleries of different lengths, bridges of various forms, and an open water pavilion are "dividing but not separating" devices that maintain the continuity of space between scenic sections. The fluidity and unity of space are further promoted by the rock-lined watercourse, extending into different sections as a unifying factor. Each scenic section is characterized by a predominance of different garden features or the same features in varied compositions. Sections 3, 6, and 7 share the same theme and identical garden features: an enclosure formed by various types of architecture and a body of water serving as a central point of interest. Changing the size and shape of the central pond and altering the arrangement of architecture and plantings create scenic sections that present refreshingly diversified views. The secluded section 4 in the northwest corner is shaped by a range of gigantic rockery at the south and east, a lofty hall at the north, and a stretch of walking gallery at the west. An extension of rockery subdivides the small enclosed courtyard into two parts and yet retains the continuity of space, thus greatly

FIG. 11.18 (top left) *The existence of a bridge greatly enhances the depth of an end-vista view of a water pavilion in the Unsuccessful Politician's Garden, Suzhou.*

FIG. 11.19 (top right) *A planting of water lilies gives a sense of distance to the watercourse; in the Summer Retreating Mountain Villa, Chengde.*

FIG. 11.20 (top left) *A walking gallery divides the space without blocking garden views. The horizontal composition of the roof, the low railing wall of the walking gallery, and the rock-lined embankment are enlivened by the vertical trees; in the Unsuccessful Politician's Garden, Suzhou.*

FIG. 11.21 (bottom) *A crooked walking gallery in the Unsuccessful Politician's Garden divides scenic sections and yet retains the continuity of the space.*

FIG. 11.22 (top right) *Looking from the inner garden of the Unsuccessful Politician's Garden to the main scenic section through an arch formed by the rockery supporting a walking gallery that meanders along with a partition wall and trellis windows. The garden is divided by walls and yet remains wonderfully united in space.*

FIG. 11.23 (top left) *A single-plank stone bridge is devised as a space divider over a watercourse; in the Pleasure Garden, Suzhou.*

FIG. 11.24 (top right) *A view of the main scenic section of the Unsuccessful Politician's Garden from the Truth-Winning Pavilion through the Little Flying Rainbow.*

FIG. 11.25 (bottom) *A courtyard is defined in space by ground that is raised in levels; in the Unsuccessful Politician's Garden, Suzhou.*

enhancing the seeming depth of the courtyard. Topside views tend to overexpose the scenic space, contradicting the attempt to make it seem appealing and spacious. In this garden, however, when seen from the elevated hall in the north of the courtyard, an inexhaustible viewing effect is provided by the lofty rockery partially concealing the southern part of the courtyard space.

The central scenic section 2, though rather limited in area, is designed with a contrast of rocky hills in the northwest and architecture in the southeast. A roofed bridge crosses the watercourse at the north. When viewed at a distance, from the halls at the south or from the crooked bridge (fig. 11.26), a part of the secluded section 5 is revealed through the roofed bridge, suggesting a larger body of water beyond what is visible. In fact, section 5 is merely a stream of water winding along a miniature valley at the northwest foot of the predominating rockery.

Two bridges break up the elongated central pond into sections, improve the proportion of both the central pond and the central scenic section, and appear to broaden the actually narrow space. When viewing from the bridge between sections 2 and 6, one can enjoy a layered garden view of seemingly infinite depth (plan 15.B, fig. 11.27).

A little courtyard garden attached to a residential house in Yangzhou (fig. 7.25g) takes up a plot measuring only 6 by 10 meters. Small as it is, the garden is clearly divided into two sections. A small den built on the north faces a tiny court not more than 2½ meters in depth. An elegant scene composed of a small rockery, a modest grove of bamboo, and a sheltering shade tree embellishes the compact space, successfully eliminating any cramped feeling. The depth of this courtyard garden is seemingly expanded through the trellised window on the divisional wall. Furthermore, a walking gallery attached to the west wall and the above-mentioned rockery at the east side both continue on to the southern section. Thus, the "divided" space of two small courtyards is once again unified as a continuous entity. The walking gallery leads upward with a ramp floor to a small enclosed pavilion built as the extension of a tiny pool's rocky embankment. This is a wonderful example of an extremely small garden that incorporates all the major garden features and yet maintains a spacious effect by skillfully applying the unfailing method: Let the space be "divided, not separated."

Appreciation of the fluidity of continuous space and an awareness of hidden space achieved through plotted guidance are common to contemporary western architectural practice. But continuous space disposition, explained here as the principle of "divided, not separated," has been practiced, summed up, and crystallized into an important heritage of Chinese garden art throughout the long history of Chinese culture.

Borrowed Scenery — Unlimited Viewing (fig. 11.28)

"Scenery borrowing" is a unique design technique profoundly applied in Chinese gardens. Natural scenic landscape and appealing neighboring or far-off architectural features can all be incorporated into the garden setting or

FIG. 11.26 (top)   *A view from the end of a crooked bridge toward a bridge mounted with a pavilion in the Studio of Mental Peace in Beihai Park, Beijing.*

FIG. 11.27 (center)   *Looking west from an arched bridge toward section 2 (plan 5) in the Studio of Mental Peace.*

FIG. 11.28 (bottom)   *Longguang Ta, the Dragon Light Pagoda, on Xi Shan is "borrowed" as part of the magnificent scenic view of the Carefree-Abiding Garden, Wuxi.*

into garden scenes. Whenever possible, the Chinese garden builder made sure to include landmarks and tall spectacles such as towering ancient pagodas, picturesque temples on lofty locations, and the silhouettes of mountain ranges.

As most private gardens are enclosed by walls, there is not much problem with environmental concerns, especially since the neighboring buildings are usually single-story. The crowns of shade trees rising from nearby courtyards, the occasional glimpse of an elegant pavilion or a segment of an adjacent house's gray-tiled roof with artistically curved eaves can serve as a foil to enhance the garden's attractiveness. Fortunately, traditional Chinese architecture maintained a consistent style, with relatively minor variations, throughout its long history. Therefore, the possibility of incongruous architectural context is less than it is elsewhere within the present architectural world.

Elevated vantage points are sometimes arranged in the form of a two-story tower, a pavilion, or a terrace built on an artificial hill commanding distance views of surrounding countryside with sparkling flooded rice fields in patched patterns or overlooking a lower neighboring attraction. As a result, the possibility of extending the scenic boundaries is greatly increased no matter what the garden's original size.

A open pavilion situated on an artificial hill, the Autumn Hill, in Ge Yuan (plan 8), gives an overall view of the peaks, cliffs, ravines, and gorges of this gigantic rockery. To the north of the garden, the vista includes the city wall, the Slender West Lake, the Level Mountain Hall, and many other "borrowed" scenic attractions of the ancient city of Yangzhou.

Investigating and incorporating natural landscape resources into garden scenes is a serious concern of Chinese garden makers. Jichang Yuan in Wuxi is another garden with an excellent location that takes advantage of being set off by beautiful mountain views, Hui Shan in the west and Xi Shan in the southeast (plan 10A). The quintessence of the natural environment is skillfully blended into its garden scenes. The Dragon Light Pagoda towering over Xi Shan can be observed through the grove of trees across the central pond and has become one of the most attractive garden views (fig. 11.28). Looking to the north from the east shore of the central pond, Wei Shan sits aloft behind the artificial hills of the garden. The natural background landscape and the garden have so intimately mingled that it is hard to tell where nature begins and where the work of humans stops. Thus, the garden's size is seemingly multiplied.

The ancient Chinese garden maker never overlooked detailed designing of garden scenes as a factor indispensable to accomplishing a successful garden. The artificial hills in Jichang Yuan were constructed with rocks excavated from Wei Shan; and as the water of the garden pond was introduced from the spring of Wei Shan, eventually the mountain became an integral part of the garden views. Thus, the garden's boundary is extended far beyond to the mountain, Wei Shan.

The Fishing Terrace, formerly called the Blower's Terrace, a pavilion built on an island in the Slender West Lake in Yangzhou, is renowned for its bor-

rowed scenes as all the best views of the lake are focused at this spot; they are framed and further enhanced by four moon gates on walls of the pavilion that face different directions (fig. 11.29).

The Dual-Delight Pavilion is in the Unsuccessful Politician's Garden at the boundary wall adjacent to the central garden (plan 1). The pavilion commands a segmental top view of the inner garden as well as borrowing magnificent water scenes from the central garden. This pavilion, itself, serves as a spectacular end vista when it is viewed from the east end of the central garden (fig. 11.30).

Space is also borrowed from the sky through the reflection of placid ponds, and the result is especially desirable in confined garden sections (fig. 11.31). Resources of borrowed scenery include views within the garden and at a distance. The pagoda on the Jade Fountain Hill thus appears, borrowed, in the views of the Summer Palace (fig. 11.32). As far as the vision ranges, favorable views are encompassed; and, of course, the unsightly is concealed.

The technique of scene borrowing is used to expand limited garden space by extending the sight range to command the best surrounding views. In practice, it intermingles constructed garden views with the natural landscape. As a result, the garden space is seemingly multiplied.

Contrast

Contrast is common to all forms of art. In garden design, it seeks to captivate viewers' attention and sustain their interest. An intensified impression is achieved by arranging a successive view, strikingly changed from that previously perceived; the intensification is based on the fact that the immediate second impression is greatly influenced by the first.

Contrasts are practiced in all aspects of garden design, including scenic themes, space disposition, form composition, texture, color, and lighting. Contrasts are presented as: large versus small, massiveness versus void space, open versus secluded, broad versus narrow, straight versus curved or crooked, massive versus dainty, dense versus sparse, vertical versus horizontal, tall versus low, distant view versus close-up, mysterious depth versus cheerful intimacy, sound versus quiet, bright versus dim (fig. 11.33), dynamic versus static, and so on.

Being built as naturalistic environments, Chinese gardens have as their fundamental scenic contrasts hills and water opposed to architecture; that is, a contrast of naturalistic features and artifacts (figs. 2.5, 10.11). As both are essential components of the garden, they are often positioned as *te-jing,* opposing vistas or counterpoints, providing refreshingly different views from one to the other. Just as the hill-and-water scene is natural beauty distilled through artistic reformation, so the garden architecture is endowed with curvilinear configuration derived from nature; with the further application of plantings and other ways of transition, there is no risk of discord or lack of harmony.

Water is used in contrast to rockery or architecture (fig. 11.34), like lightness versus heaviness, void space versus solid mass, and also as moving and romantic versus still and staid. With the mirroring effect of a water surface, harmony among these contrasting elements is unfailing.

The gate of a private garden is usually modest in scale and unremarkable in design (fig. 11.35), consistent with the garden's placid mood. Moreover, as the gate is the beginning of the trip to the garden, this is an execution of an important principle of space design: "to confine before opening." The humble gate is meant to contrast with the elegance and spaciousness of the garden proper in order to procure an intensifying effect.

The entrance to the Lingering Garden in Suzhou shows the remarkable wit

of its designer, who turned the unfortunate condition of a narrow access to the street into a way of forming an interesting contrast — both in space and brightness of lighting — with the garden's main scenic section (fig. 11.36). The lengthy and uninteresting lane is broken into smaller spaces of varied proportions. Daylight is introduced here through tiny courts of different size and shape in a subdued way and yet with obvious variation in intensity. All this not only diminishes the monotony of the linear itinerary, but creates a masterpiece of space disposition leading to the gallery before the Crisscrossing Ancient Tree Branches Court. Here, a visual climax of the garden's main scenic attraction is revealed with contrasting spaciousness and sunlit brightness (plan 3).

It has been asserted that the Chinese garden is curvilinear in nature and that the straight line is taboo. In fact, curved and straight lines coexist naturally in Chinese gardens, and the curved lines appear more amiable and cognizable when contrasted with straight lines and vice versa. The occasional appearance of straight passages does add enchanting views as well (fig. 11.17).

Visual Deception

The Chinese garden is denounced by some connoisseurs as a garden of deception, a small world of make-believe. But the enchanting ways of deception help to expand the space of confined urban lots. When a half pavilion or the segment of another type of building is attached to the boundary or divisional wall (figs. 11.8, 11.11), one can scarcely penetrate the fraud from a distance. In this most audacious architectural approach, a structure portrays only a segment of a sizable and elaborately embellished pavilion, allowing the observer's assumption to complete the unbuilt portion. Thus, the garden plot seems to extend far beyond its actual boundary.

Occasionally, a tiny inner court is endowed with a decorative door opening that suggests a larger space within the entry. Winding paths or a streamlet leading to a mere corner of the garden are often presented in deceitful ways to suggest a larger mysterious, hidden space (figs. 11.37, 11.38).

The mirroring effect of water surface is another deceitful measure that doubles the height of all garden features arranged around or at a pond (fig. 11.39). To take advantage of numerous wall openings that reveal segments of garden scenes beyond the wall, mirrors may be attached to boundary walls or to the back wall of a pavilion. The views reflected in the mirror make viewers believe in the existence of scenic space beyond the wall.

Using plants with larger leaves and brilliant deep-green colors as the foreground, and different plants with leaves of smaller sizes and lighter color arranged in diminishing sequence, lends greater depth to the scenic composition (fig. 11.40). The plantain tree and the canna, with spectacular large leaves, are favored as foreground plantings. Different bamboo species of various sizes are sometimes arranged with the small-leaved bamboos at the background and the large-leaved ones in the foreground. This promotes a make-believe perspective, giving the illusion of a larger area while actually encompassing a smaller space.

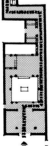

FIG. 11.35 (top left) *A simple but elegant gate is characteristic of private gardens, to contrast with magnificent garden views; the gate of the Surging-Wave Pavilion garden, Suzhou.*

FIG. 11.36 (left) *Plan of the entry to the Lingering Garden, Suzhou.*

FIG. 11.37 (top right) *Mysterious paths merely lead the way for a side trip into a corner of a garden, but they falsely suggest more space hidden out of sight.*

FIG. 11.38 (above) *A rockery built against a boundary wall. A tunnel purposely gives an "endless" look to the watercourse in the Slender West lake, Yangzhou.*

FIG. 11.39 (top)   *A solitary rockery display in the central pond of the Lion Grove garden, Suzhou. The mirroring effect of the water surface doubles the height of the rockery.*

FIG. 11.40 (bottom)   *A water scene in the Ancient Magnificent Garden, Shanghai. Plants with large leaves are often used as the foreground.*

A similar method is used in arranging architecture. Buildings are constructed in diminishing sizes from important viewing points to induce an illusion of greater distance (fig. 11.18). Therefore, pavilions on artificial hills are always highly reduced in scale, not only to avoid an overpowering effect on the hills but also to create a seemingly greater distance in the garden according the above-mentioned effect.

As far as details are concerned, when a hill of modest height is constructed, the rise of its steps is often reduced to 2 or 3 inches. If people climb more steps when ascending, they think the hill is much loftier than its actual height. Sometimes, basically level ground is covered with natural rocks and a complementary use of plants in an attempt to convince beholders that they are in a mountainous environment.

In fact, the methods of diminishing scale, borrowing scenes, and concealing the enclosure are all fascinating and effective visual deceptions that assist in creating seeming spaciousness in a limited area.

CHAPTER TWELVE

Dynamic Viewing: Design for Four Seasons and Five Senses

The Chinese garden is not merely a universally appreciated three-dimensional painting; it is also a four-dimensional time-space presentation. Beholders gradually become aware of these dimensions while moving in sequential spaces, following planned touring routes, over a period of time. This cumulative visual perception leads to a dramatic effect on the viewer through mobile viewing, which cannot be compared to ordinary static-viewing experiences. All this has been discussed in Chapter Ten, but dynamic viewing of the Chinese garden further includes "views outside the view," which means that the views change not only with "every step forward" but with the seasons, weather, times of day, age of the plantings, and even the beholder's mood. Thus, Chinese gardens are always attractive and fresh to visitors no matter how many times they have seen the same garden.

One special charm of garden art is that it consists of living elements which change with the season and the age of the plantings. Chinese gardens are exquisitely planned to capitalize on the dynamic beauty of varying weather and different times of day. Another unique aesthetic quality highly valued in the Chinese garden is an air of antiquity presented chiefly through old trees of artistic posture, grotesque weatherworn rockeries, and the display of historical literary inscriptions (fig. 9.11). All these charms can be acquired only with the aging of a garden through the centuries.

Four Seasons

Utilizing seasonal changes of plants to create perennial variation of the landscape is a fundamental approach to dynamic viewing in the Chinese garden. Different kinds of plants bring out the diversity of garden views through their characteristic posture, texture, color, odor, and even the acoustic effects they generate. As the seasons go by, they put forth leaves, flowers, and fruits. Even the process of shedding leaves and flower petals, and eventually presenting bare branches, is attractive to the Chinese (fig. 12.1).

Magnolia beside most main halls of the garden, forsythia along the embankments, and peonies on the parterres are cultivated for early and late spring views; lotus and crepe myrtle are planted for summer scenes; chrysanthemum and red maple are meant for autumn delight; and the camellia, nandina, and plum blossom are dedicated to winter enjoyment.

When dealing with a composite cultivation of different plants, it is important to achieve balanced presentation with varying centers of interest during different seasons of the year, depending on when the plants sprout and flower and when the color of their leaves changes. The dramatic changes of deciduous trees and flowering plants are especially rewarding; they lend variety when the growth of their leaves and the time for blossoming are integrated into scenic design.

Many of the celebrated gardens have special scenes for different seasons. The Net Master's Garden incorporates scenic views dedicated to different seasons arranged around a central pond (plan 2, fig. 12.2). The Duck-Shooting Gallery and the Half Pavilion command a spring view to the south, an aged wisteria drooping over a yellow stone rockery. The Water Pavilion for Washing Headgear String, to the south of the pond, is a vantage point that looks toward the Watching Pines and Appreciating Paintings Studio (fig. 12.3). This pavilion is shady and cooling, especially designed for summer delight (fig. 12.2). The Moon-Arriving and Wind-Coming Pavilion, built on a raised rock terrain looking over the central pond (fig. 12.4a, b), was intended for moon watching. It was meant for special visits at the midautumn festival, to enjoy the enchanting reflection of the full moon on the placid pond. The Watching Pines and Appreciating Paintings Studio was designed for the garden's winter scenes with a foreground of aged evergreen pines, cypress, and yew planted on the parterres beside the hall to set off the snow scene (fig. 12.3).

Ge Yuan Garden in Yangzhou is noted for its gorgeous artificial hills depicting the four seasons (plan 8). The Spring View is composed of bamboo groves and "stone bamboo shoots" on two sizable parterres flanking the garden gate (fig. 5.3). The "stone bamboo shoots" are pillarlike rocks with a texture of

(a)

(b)

FIG. 12.1 (top left)   *In winter, the leafless branches of plants with graceful posture are enjoyable in a rock-plant composition.*

FIG. 12.2 (top right)   *The Water Pavilion for Washing Headgear String in the Net Master's Garden, Suzhou, is meant for summer enjoyment.*

FIG. 12.3 (center)   *Framed view of the Watching Pines and Appreciating Paintings Studio in the Net Master's Garden.*

FIG. 12.4 (bottom)   *Scenes from the Net Master's Garden: (a) viewing from A Branch Beyond the Bamboo Studio toward the Water Pavilion for Washing Headgear String and the Moon-Arriving and Wind-Coming Pavilion; (b) the framed view of the pavilion, Moon-Arriving and Wind-Coming. The inner garden is screened by the walking gallery attached to a wall.*

rough scales resembling gigantic bamboo shoots. Another rockery composition, entitled Animal Greeting the Spring, is right behind the gate.

The Summer Hill, to the west of the garden's central pond, is made of gray lake rocks (fig. 12.5). A crooked stone bridge, elevated over the water surface, leads into a mysterious cave under the hill. This cave, half submerged in the pond, is a shaded, cooling summer attraction.

The Autumn Hill, built with yellow granite, is embellished with winding paths leading up to a pavilion that perches on the peak for far-reaching viewing (fig. 12.6). Autumn is acknowledged in Chinese tradition as the best season for distance viewing through the clear sky and transparent air.

In the southeast corner of the garden, the Winter Hill presents a snow-covered rockery scene constructed with *xuan* rocks (fig. 12.7). This rock is a kind of silicone that glistens under the sunlight with a white tint, resembling a coat of snow. The enchantment of the Winter Hill is further enhanced by the acoustic effect. Circular openings with a diameter of 1 foot were made in the north wall behind the Winter Hill (plan 8). A roaring sound resembling the chilly winter wind is generated when the prevailing wind blows through the holes. This adds a dramatic feeling of chill to the winter scene. The openings also provide glimpses of the Spring Hill behind the wall, forecasting the advent of the cheerful, lively spring right after the severe, freezing winter. Here, a landscape view is also meant to encourage people in a symbolic way to stand firm against temporary hardship. The Chinese garden is, thus, as thought provoking as any other form of art.

The Thirty-Six Mandarin Ducks Hall in the inner garden of the Unsuccessful Politician's Garden is subdivided into two rooms that face north and south, respectively, and are designed with absolutely different tones (plan 1). The southern hall is warmed—both in temperature and atmosphere—with ample sunshine for winter comfort. The northern hall, devoid of sunshine, has an exceptionally peaceful cooling tone, provided by a view of sun-brightened lotus blossoms swaying over a shaded water surface outside the north window. Physically and aesthetically, this is indeed an ideal summer retreat.

Time and Weather

The changes of weather and different times of the day are important in dynamic viewing. The special charm of viewing in the rain is deeply appreciated. Walking galleries were erected to connect buildings so that people could tour in the rain without getting wet. Being protected from the weather also promotes the enjoyment of a snow scene during winter, a blossoming lotus scene under the scorching midsummer sun, as well as allowing the beholder to participate in a beloved, melancholy rainy scene.

Water pavilions dedicated to the lotus scene are built over the watercourse, close enough for the raindrops to be seen dancing upon lotus leaves swaying in the breeze. In many gardens, water pavilions were also intended for enjoying romantic night scenes with the reflection of the moon and moonlight. Two viewing points called the Crescent Terraces were built in Roar-Resounding Mountain Villa, Yangzhou (plan 9), along the two-story double walking

FIG. 12.5 (top) *The Summer Hill in the Bamboo Leaves Garden, Yangzhou, built with lake rocks.*

FIG. 12.6 (center) *The Autumn Hill in the Bamboo Leaves Garden, built with yellow granite.*

FIG. 12.7 (bottom) *The Winter Hill in the Bamboo Leaves Garden, built with* xuan *rocks that have a coat of white tint, resembling a coat of snow.*

179

galleries, oriented in different directions. Each terrace is specially located for the pleasure of watching the moon's rise and descent.

A hall in the Summer Palace, Beijing, Hu-Shan-Zhen-Ying, True View of the Lake and Hill, is situated—as its title implies—so that viewers observe the glamorous setting sun backlighting the "borrowed view" of the graceful Western Hills in the distance (fig. 11.32).

The beauty of changing views is further intensified by reflections in the placid water surface, set off by varying lights and colors of the sky during different times of day. Great value in setting off garden views is placed upon the dynamic beauty of changing clouds and their reflections in water surfaces.

The daily rise and fall of the tide changes the water level, alternately hiding and revealing garden features arranged around or at a pond—rocky islets or artistically designed embankments. For example, changes of water level can lend quite different looks to a linear watercourse, ranging from a flooding brook to a romantic, threadlike streamlet, when the watercourse is designed with an appropriate V-shaped cross-section—that is, broader at the top and narrower at the bottom of the water bed.

Light, Shade, and Shadow

Deliberate attempts are made to provide enjoyment of sunlight and moonlight. Screened sunlight or moonlight create an atmosphere of serenity that Chinese garden makers eagerly sought. The golden rays of the morning sun filtered through a bamboo grove, resembling a magnificent golden screen because the fine bamboo leaves are so daintily transparent. Remarkable shadows cast on whitewashed walls are designed to enrich the garden views (fig. 12.8). Whitewashed walls often serve to capture the shadows of several stalks of bamboo, some rockery, or a quaint plant in sunlight. Moving shadows on courtyards or pathways are considered more interesting than the static patterns of pavings (fig. 12.9). Shadows of the bare branches of deciduous trees quivering in the breeze or traveling with the pleasant winter sunlight are captivating over a sculptured relief.

A shrouding of the dark shadow cast by an aged wisteria is favored in Chinese gardens for its purifying visual pleasure and its physical cooling effect (fig. 12.10). When the sparkling sunlight finds its way into the heavily shaded bosquet of pine trees, another form of moving pattern—a negative version—is created.

Being consistent with a love of elegance, artificial lighting is used in Chinese gardens to accentuate the scenic attractions. The lighted nocturnal scene, the "lantern display," of the Net Master's Garden in Suzhou is a special event for garden lovers. In the Summer Palace, walls attached to a walking gallery enclosing the outer courtyard of Le Shou Tang, Happiness-Longevity Hall, are adorned with window openings in fanciful shapes. Lights were placed in these windows during night boating parties. These lights and their reflections on the Kunming Lake produced a most romantic night scene.

FIG. 12.8 (top) *A grove of bamboos focused on a window opening is enchanting with its moving shadows.*

FIG. 12.9 (bottom left) *The pattern of the railing of a bridge enhanced by its shadow, a bridge leading to the entry of Fish-Watching Flower Harbor in the West lake, Hangzhou.*

FIG. 12.10 (bottom right) *A wisteria-covered trellis built on a bridge provides a cooling rest stop in the summer; in the Lingering Garden, Suzhou.*

Birds, Fish, and Insects

The earliest gardens of the ancient Chinese emperors were founded to preserve and breed animal life for hunting purposes. As the later gardens diminished in size and became more culturally oriented, animal life began to disappear in Chinese gardens. Unfortunately, deer and cranes, once cherished as symbols of longevity and blessing for the prosperity of offspring, can no longer be found in traditional Chinese gardens; but the Park of Nara in Japan keeps the old tradition of domesticating deer as a special attraction.

Fish, birds, and insects are noticeably important elements in the existing gardens. Gold carps are loved and widely bred in small and large ponds, or even in vases of different sizes half buried in courtyard gardens. Water pavilions and crooked bridges over the water are ideal for the contemplation of fish (fig. 10.19). A scenic spot along the West Lake in Hangzhou, Hua-Gong-Gua-Yu, the Fish-Watching Flower Harbor, makes a specialty of harboring thousands of goldfish.

The singing of cicadas and crickets accentuates the seasonal changes of luxuriant summer days and quiescent autumn nights. Flower beds are cultivated to attract butterflies and bees. Multifarious butterfly shapes and colors and the buzzing music of the bees delight the beholder, as does the enchantment of their movement among the blossoms. In fulfilling spiritual satisfaction, the eagerness of butterflies and bees dancing around the flowers further symbolizes perpetual love.

Mandarin ducks swimming in couples, embellish the watercourses with their gorgeous feathers and graceful movements, and are favored as a blessing for devoted marriage. Since birds, fish, and insects were popular subjects for traditional Chinese paintings, Chinese gardens served as ideal places for artistic creation.

The rings of ripples caused by a streamlet plopping into the corner of a pond, or even by a tiny water insect skiing over the surface, are perceived as great beauty to be enjoyed in a pond of still water. The occasional singing of birds and insects most effectively enhances the serenity of a forested hill. Moreover, it is only in such a background of extreme peace and quietness that their exquisiteness could be appreciated. Relativity is profoundly and ingeniously practiced in the art of Chinese gardens. Tranquillity and stillness are essential for contrasting delicate movements and enjoying their dynamic beauty. The movements are subtle, perceivable only in a placid background.

Design for Five Senses

The Chinese garden does not strive for visual pleasure alone. Satisfaction of the "five senses" is meant to be provided. Acoustic and olfactory satisfaction play an indispensable part in garden design.

Serenity is the main source of ancient Chinese poems, which were mostly expressions of unworldly thought, solitude, and poetic feelings. Tranquillity can be sensed and appreciated only when contrasted with the mild sound generated through various media, while absolute silence leads only to emptiness in spirit. Therefore, the cultivation of plant life in the Chinese garden is not restricted to judicious appreciation of shape, color, and texture. The acoustic properties and the odors activated by rain and wind are also expected to enhance the quality of scenic environment. Plants with spectacularly large leaves, such as plantain trees, are often planted right next to the window of a den, forming an enchanting "window scene." Moreover, the clattering of the leaves swaying in the wind and the noise of raindrops beating down on them are also planned attractions. The finer leaves of bamboo and the needles of pine trees generate different pitches of tone when set in motion. The sighing of the wind or splashing of the rain in a pine or bamboo grove garnishes a Chinese garden with the appealing solitary atmosphere of a remote valley in the mountains.

Chinese gardens not only "borrow" landscape views from the vicinity but also strive to exploit whatever neighboring acoustical delights are available. Nan-Ping-Wan-Zhong, the Late Bell of the South Screen, was one of the Ten Scenic Views of the West Lake in Hangzhou. The chiming of temple bells in the vicinity was incorporated, for the sake of sentimental satisfaction, as part of the landscape attraction.

Acoustical fantasies have been executed since ancient times. The Rill of Eight Musical Tones in the Carefree-Abiding Garden in Wuxi was a stream of water falling from different heights upon stones of different sizes, shapes, and densities. These stones were manipulated as resonance boards to play eight musical tones (fig. 12.11). There was no splashing or roaring, as in an exciting waterfall, but merely mild stimulation that harmonized with the tranquillity of the garden entity. Unfortunately, the Rill of Eight Musical Tones needs restoration in order to manifest its original charm.

Another masterpiece of acoustical design is found in Jixiao Shanzhuang (plan 9). A spectacular pavilion was built to function as a stage that seemed to float at one end of the central pond, leaving a large portion of placid water surface as the sound-reflecting board for the musical or theatrical performances on the stage (fig. 7.21). Two-story walking galleries, half surrounding the central pond, and the pavilion stage, functioned as balconies for the audience. Dividing walls were built along the center line of the galleries, forming most impressive two-story double galleries. In ancient China, women were forbidden to contact the male-dominated world; they were kept at the rear of the double galleries and were supposed to enjoy the performances through grilled openings of the dividing wall whenever guests were present. This architectural complex is an outstanding example of how well the scenic components accommodated sophisticated functional needs in Chinese gardens.

Water surfaces that actually constitute sounding boards add greatly to the serenity and poetic moods of the Chinese gardens. Besides, the tinkling streamlets, with their sound and movements, are often used as an effective enticement for visiting hidden garden scenes. Water, as the only moving element aside from the animal life, plays an important role in the Chinese garden's dynamic beauty.

FIG. 12.11 (left) *The Rill of Eight Musical Tones in the Carefree-Abiding Garden, Wuxi, has its title inscribed on the rock.*

FIG. 12.12 (right) *Sweet osmanthus is a favorite planting for a small court in front of a hall or studio; in the Net Master's Garden, Suzhou.*

Plants intended for olfactory pleasure are carefully located for the best results. Sweet osmanthus and gardenias are loved for their strong fragrance. They are best planted in courtyards and other compact scenic enclosures (fig. 12.12). Man Ju Long, a scenic valley in Hangzhou, Zhejiang Province, was a famous autumn attraction with the osmanthus in full bloom. Its basinlike site was ideal for sustaining the fragrance, and there was adequate sunshine and humidity for the growth and blossoming of osmanthus. Unfortunately, this attraction needs to be restored.

For best results, fragrant plants are carefully located in relation to the buildings they adorn (fig. 7.5). The plantings are often placed windward of the buildings, according to the prevailing winds of the blossoming season, to ensure that their fragrance is fully conveyed into the buildings by the breeze. To prevent desensitization, it is important to place plantings at a moderate distance from the buildings, with the fragrance strengthened by occasional breezes.

Sweet osmanthus was sometimes censured as too strong and vulgar for the sophisticated taste of the ancient Chinese gentlemen scholars. The Chinese orchid, lotus, magnolia, and other flowering plants with mild fragrance are preferred. But when the pleasant odor is intended to attract the visitor's attention to garden scenes before they are actually disclosed, plants with strong fragrance, such as the sweet osmanthus, are the better choice.

Gardens are also a place for wine drinking and tea sipping. Plants that bear fruits and have edible leaves, flowers, or roots are planted to feast the taste buds. Seasonal changes are enjoyed not only through visual perception but with a supply of special delicacies harvested from the plantings in different seasons throughout the year. Powdered lotus root sauce and iced water chestnut cake, scented with sweetened osmanthus blossoms, are prepared as summer refreshments. Tea chrysanthemum blossoms are dehydrated to serve as a healthy, cooling drink. Sweet osmanthus wine was brewed to celebrate the Midautumn Festival. More plants, too numerous to be listed, are included in gardens for scents and herbs as well as for visual pleasure.

Garden features within the reach of humans — such as architectural components, detailed to the molding of door and window frames, or the texture of the barks of trees — are all exquisitely devised to provide tactile satisfaction. Furthermore, the varied sensations obtained from weather and temperature changes are traditionally prized. Even the experience of being moistened by the morning dew is taken as a sentimental fulfillment, repeatedly praised in poems. The Chinese garden is indeed ingeniously designed for the "four seasons" and "five senses."

Epilogue

Chinese garden art has been a popular topic lately. A number of gardens have been built in different continents during the last few years. The first Chinese garden built abroad in modern times was Ming Xuan, the Astor Court, in the Metropolitan Museum of Art, New York City, in 1980. This indoor garden is a replica of an inner garden, the Late Spring Studio, of the Net Master's Garden, Suzhou. In 1983, Fanghua Yuan, the Fragrant Flower Garden, was presented to the Sixteenth International Garden Fair in Munich, Germany. In 1984, Yianxiu Yuan, the Swallow Beauty Garden, was built in Liverpool, England. It reproduces a scenic section of Jingxin Zhai, the Studio of Mental Peace, Beihai Park, Beijing. Successively, many more authentic Chinese classical gardens were created and maintained in Canada, Australia, many European countries, and Africa.

These gardens were prefabricated in China with Chinese rocks, plants, wood components, bricks, and tiles; they were then shipped to their destinations, to be assembled on site. The aim was precise accuracy of replication. High standards of craftsmanship were maintained in presenting the typical styles, whether of the private or the imperial garden. People all over the world can enjoy this unique form of garden art without the trouble of an international journey. However, these gardens were costly both to construct and to maintain. The cost of a single project might reach as high as 10 million U.S. dollars. It is clear that the construction of such gardens must be sponsored by foundations or governmental funds as an international cultural exchange.

Chinese traditional garden art grew from the unique physical and cultural contexts of ancient China and evolved through centuries to its culmination in a mature style. When put into an alien environmental context, these masterpieces were apt to be seen as an exotic attraction of museum collections rather than as part of the history of architectural evolution. The construction of Chinese gardens in European countries during the seventeenth and eighteenth centuries may be the precursor of the current enthusiasm.

Gardens, as living art, are best composed with local material, especially the plants, not merely for enhanced survival and economics but for the stimulation of artistic innovation.

While writing this book on Chinese garden design, I designed a Chinese garden in a college campus in Lincoln, Nebraska. I did not stress authenticity but saw this presentation as a way of introducing Chinese garden art to a midwestern U.S. state. I was also attempting to cross-influence the art of another country for the enrichment of modern garden practice. The site being very small, reminiscent of an enlarged *bonzai,* the "scale" was carefully treated: Small plants were selected, small both in overall size and in individual leaves and branches. First of all, of course, I chose hardy plants naturalized to the local climate. The California lava rock gratifyingly resembles the Chinese Taihu lake rock in color and texture and is light and handy for construction. When selected and utilized with oriental criteria for form and composition, the lava rock had a suitable "Chinese look" but was available at a local nursery at market price.

In most traditional gardens, rocks are often sculptured and molded together to form stately artificial hills. Due to the severe Nebraska winters, however, the disintegration of the molded hills would be inevitable. Therefore, rocks were displayed singly in this garden. Water is indispensable to Chinese gardens, but the seasons for running fountains in Lincoln, Nebraska, are very short; thus a dry pond with a white river rock surface, representing the water, was chosen to contrast with the greenery.

As garden architecture is an essential component in Chinese gardens, a feature such as a small open pavilion could be most attractive and very Chinese. Many of the newly built hotels in China are adorned with colorful pavilions, having pointed eaves, in spite of their modern architectural settings. In designing this garden, an important consideration was to harmonize it with the college campus. I felt that any architecture strongly Chinese in character, attractive as the feature might be, would not blend into the background of an occidental campus. Therefore, a simple wood-plank bridge was built as the only garden architecture.

Grass lawn is not much used in traditional Chinese gardens; but since the area of the garden is small and the garden is entirely exposed to the campus, grass is used to tie it to the campus entity. A Scotch pine with asymmetrical branches was purchased from a local nursery at a discount price because of its "unhealthy" look. The pine stands for the familiar symbol of the Chinese landscape, the "welcoming guest pine," introducing the novel beauty of artistic asymmetry into an occidental setting. Throughout this project, I emphasized and tried to express my opinion of adapting Chinese garden design theory and methodology instead of using simple imitation and reproduction.

It was most disappointing, however, to travel around the world finding identical cities and architecture in different countries or different regions within a country. In my experience, in traveling in two of the youngest and largest developed countries in the world, the United States and Australia, distinctive identities of the cities are hardly conceivable. There are no substantial characteristics to differentiate these nations architecturally. The use of modern technology seems to be the reason for this. The availability of speedy and efficient means of communication and internationally wide admiration for prominent architects' styles comprise the more immediate causes. But the world would be much more beautiful if different countries presented varied, original architecture.

The pioneers of modern architecture made great progress in architectural history, meeting people's changing functional needs with an unprecedented construction speed, utilizing advanced science and technology. Mies van de Rohe fulfilled his historical mission with his solution of using glass-veiled metal structure, subtly proportioned in form and refined in details. His revolutionary enthusiasm greatly contributed to a novel architectural episode, leaving to posterity the search for harmony and historical continuity between modern architecture and the existing environment.

In China during the 1950s, with the drastically increasing demand for mass building construction, the limited supply of such conventional building materials as brick and timber could no longer satisfy the needs. By the late 1950s, the addition of new steel and cement factories ensured a supply of concrete slabs; from then on, the flat roof replaced the traditional pitched roof. Through conscientious effort, the use of reinforced concrete frame structure could have brought back the advantages and aesthetic characteristics of the traditional timber frame structure. To the contrary, with the impact of the western modern architectural movement, the "international style" began to show up in China. Fortunately, and unfortunately, the Chinese, with a strong emotional appeal for their historical tradition, demanded a national expression. Nevertheless, the right demand ended in a wrong solution. The revival of classic Chinese architecture prevailing in the mid-1950s led to the costly construction of heavily molded concrete curved roofs to reproduce the lightweight timber roof structures. Sheer imitation of forms was not only beyond the budget allotted to the majority of architectural projects, but it infringed on the tradition of logical and rational beauty demanded in Chinese architecture. With the lessons learned from searching for a national architecture for over 30 years, the Chinese began to recognize that their architectural heritage, the basis of modern practice, lies in the traditional garden juxtaposed with the vernacular architecture of China.

In western practice, Frank Lloyd Wright's striving for an organic relationship with the natural environment was carried out mainly by means of stretching single buildings horizontally to mingle with landscape settings (fig. E.1). His organic architecture was very successful in rural contexts, but better ways of incorporating architecture with densely built urban contexts, for a more harmonious and naturalistic environment, still have to be explored.

Traditional Chinese gardens were more or less constructed living environments that excelled in creating miniature naturalistic worlds within cities, in spite of all the stringent limitations (fig. E.2). Chinese garden design has a

FIG. E.1 (top) *Frank Lloyd Wright indicated Falling Water's organic relationship with the natural environment by stretching a single building horizontally.*

FIG. E.2 (bottom) *The Chinese garden is a composition of groups of buildings incorporated with void spaces, mingled with a natural environment or built within wall enclosures in cities as "another world" that does not intrude on the environment. A top view of the main scenic section of the Net Master's Garden, Suzhou.*

valuable heritage of dealing with the continuous space composition of clustered buildings, courts, and yards. It presents a physical environment with spiritual appeal, without hampering the harmonious unity of the existing contexts. Its method of incorporating natural landscape resources—as well as urban scenic spots, far and near—can be used to expand space, to make it look as if it has no observable boundary.

A search for a refuge from busy, noisy urban pollution and an admiration for the unpolluted natural environment led to universal migration to rural areas, starting in the midtwentieth century. However, an immediate back flow of centrifugal movement to the urban areas has begun since the 1970s. We see a perpetual demand for a quiet and landscaped living environment without the loss of the urban convenience. Therefore, the principles and methodology underlying the Chinese garden are particularly worthy of reference for modern practice.

People with diversified cultural traditions and aesthetics enjoy their own forms and styles of art. Also, these characteristic forms are fascinating and attractive to people from the rest of the world. But mere appreciation of forms could not make conscientious professionals complacent. And, being discontent with the current trends toward merely adding traditional details and ornamentation to buildings in a search for human identification and as a gesture of paying homage to our heritage, we might as well endeavor, in seeking cross-cultural references, to be enriched through discovering the roots of different countries' architectural originality. Since we all have the desire to create a beautiful, innovative world, we should certainly find it valuable to explore the basic ideas, principles, and methods underlying celebrated Chinese gardens in hopes of enriching the structure of our present-day living environment.

Plans of Famous Gardens

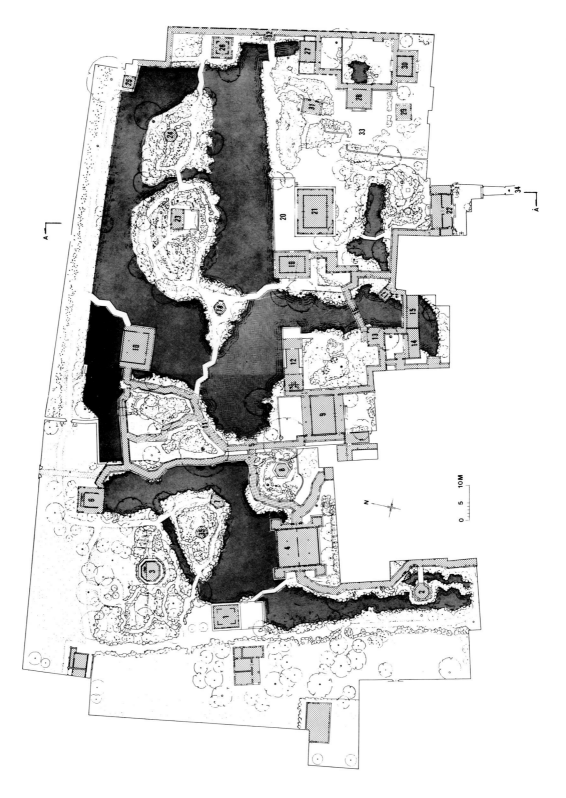

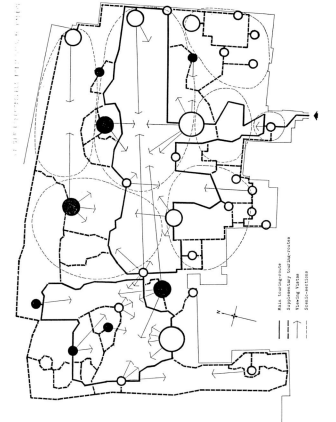

PLAN 1.A   *Zhuozheng Yuan,*
            the Unsuccessful Politician's
            Garden (Suzhou)

1. Linger and Listen Tower
2. Pagoda Reflection Pavilion
3. Floating Green Tower
4. Thirty-Six Mandarin Ducks Hall
5. Leading to a New World, pavilion
6. Reflection Mansion
7. Whom I Sit with Studio, pavilion
8. Dual-Delight Pavilion
9. Magnolia Hall
10. Mountain View Mansion
11. Willow-Shaded Winding Path, walking gallery
12. Fragrant Island, boatlike house
13. Truth-Winning Pavilion
14. Pure Will and Far-Reaching Mind, studio
15. Little Surging Wave, enclosed water pavilion
16. Little Flying Rainbow, roofed bridge
17. Pines and Breezes Pavilion
18. Lotus Breezes from All Sides Pavilion
19. Leaning Jade Studio
20. Terrace
21. Distant Fragrance Hall
22. Gate Hall
23. Fragrant Snow and Azure Sky Pavilion
24. North Hill Pavilion
25. Green Ripple Pavilion
26. Dwelling Amidst Parasol Trees and Bamboos, pavilion
27. Spring Home of Begonia
28. Dainty Hall
29. Honored Guest Pavilion
30. Listening to the Rain Studio, pavilion
31. Embroidery Pavilion
32. Leaning to the Rainbow, gate
33. Loquat Garden
34. Entry
35. Bamboo Hat Pavilion

PLAN 1.B   *Scenic Sections and Touring*
            Routes of the Unsuccessful
            Politician's Garden

Main touring-route
Supplementary touring-routes
Viewing Vistas
Scenic-sections

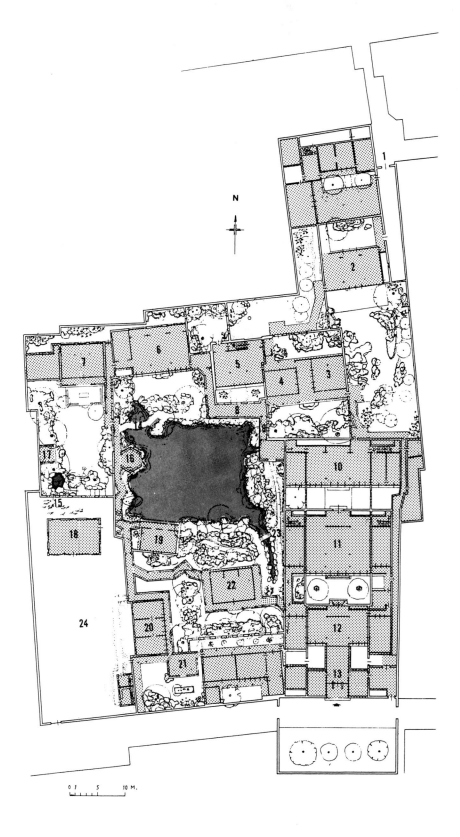

N

0 1   5   10 M.

PLAN 2 *Wangshi Yuan,*
the Net Master's Garden (Suzhou)

1. Gate
2. Cloud Ladder Chamber
3. Five-Peak Studio (ground floor)
4. Appreciating Paintings Attic (first floor)
5. Void-Collecting Studio
6. Watching Pines and Appreciating Paintings Studio
7. Late Spring Studio
8. A Branch Beyond the Bamboo Studio
9. Duck-Shooting Gallery
10. Grace-Gathering Mansion
11. Main Hall
12. Sedan Hall
13. Main Entrance
14. Plain stone bridge
15. Greenery Fountain
16. Moon-Arriving and Wind-Coming Pavilion
17. Cool Fountain Pavilion
18. Greenhouse
19. Water Pavilion for Washing Headgear String
20. Stick to Peace Hall
21. Music Chamber
22. Small Hill with Osmanthus Groves Studio
23. Arched bridge
24. Nursery

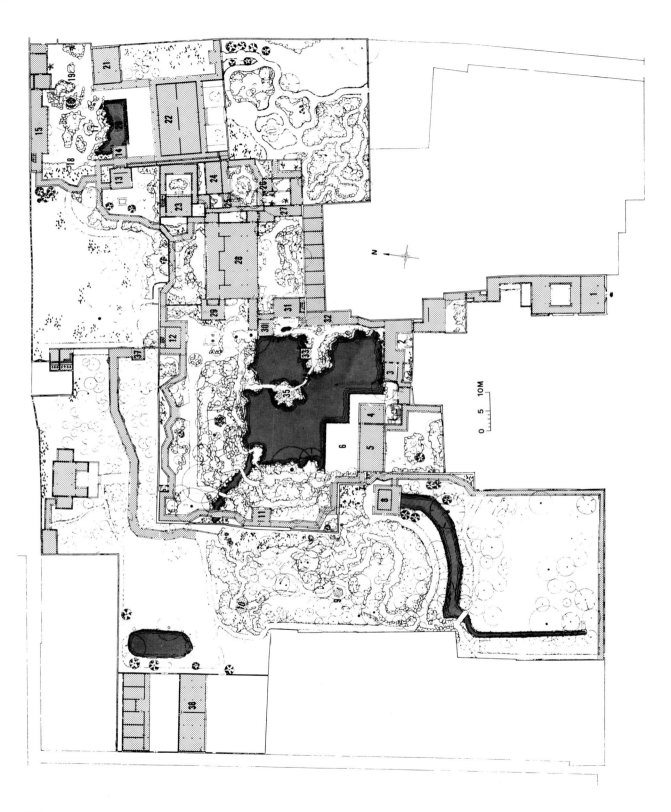

PLAN 3 *Liu Yuan,*
the Lingering Garden (Suzhou)

1. Entrance
2. Crisscrossing Ancient Tree Branches Court
3. Green Shade, water pavilion
4. Bright Zither Mansion
5. Greenery Mountain House
6. Terrace
7. Another World
8. Lively Region, hall
9. Pavilion for Free Whistling
10. Utmost Joy Pavilion
11. Osmanthus Fragrance-Smelling Studio
12. Distant Green Tower
13. Pavilion for Fine Days, Happy Rains, and Delightful Snow
14. Crest-Cloud Terrace
15. Crest-Cloud Mansion
16. Crest-Cloud Pavilion
17. Crest-Cloud Peak
18. Emerging-Cloud Peak
19. Blessing-Cloud Peak
20. Cloud-Washing Pond
21. Awaiting-the-Clouds Hut
22. Respectables of the Forests and Fountains Hall
23. Place Returned to Me for Study, studio
24. Bowing-to-the-Peak Studio
25. Viewing in Repose, gallery
26. Hut in the Stone Forest
27. Home of Cranes
28. Five-Peak Immortal Hall
29. Place for Obtaining Rope to Draw from Antiquity
30. Waterside Hall of Fresh Breezes
31. West Mansion
32. Meandering-Stream Mansion
33. Moated Pavilion
34. Wisteria Trellis
35. Little Immortal Island
36. Satisfaction Pavilion
37. Another Village
38. Greenhouse

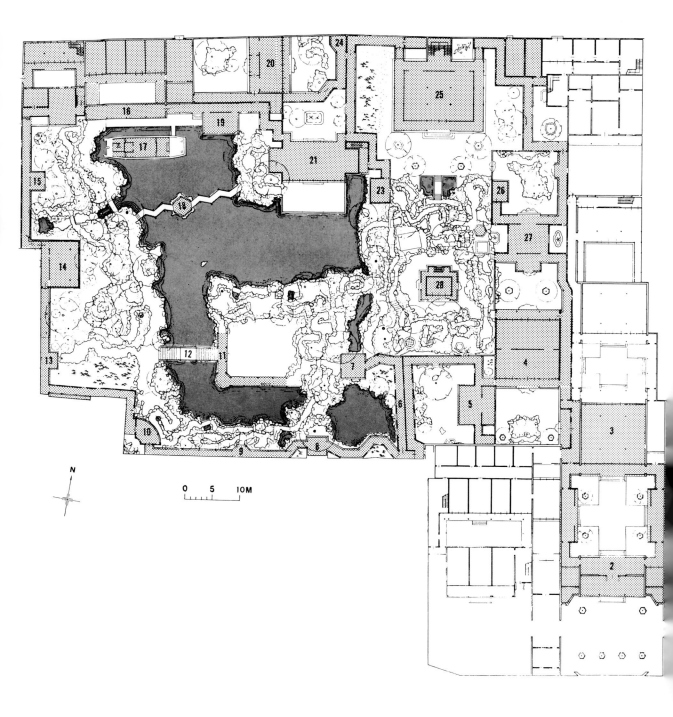

N

0   5   10M

Shizi Lin,
the Lion Grove (Suzhou)

1. Entry
2. Gate Hall
3. Ancestral Temple
4. Renowned Hall of Swallows
5. Standing-in-Snow Hall
6. Double Gallery
7. Graceful Bamboo Tower
8. Imperial Tablet Pavilion
9. Pavilion for Wen Tianxiang's Tablet
10. Fan Pavilion
11. Wisteria Trellis
12. Bridge
13. Double Fragrance Immortal Hall
14. Tower for Visiting Plum Blossoms
15. Flying-Waterfall Pavilion
16. Mansion of Faint Fragrance and Scattered Shadows
17. Stone Boatlike House
18. Lake Center Pavilion
19. True Delight Pavilion
20. Five Ancient Pines Garden
21. Lotus Hall
22. Terrace
23. Mountain View Mansion
24. Half Pavilion
25. Pointing-Cypress Studio
26. Pavilion
27. Little Square Hall
28. Lying-Cloud Chamber

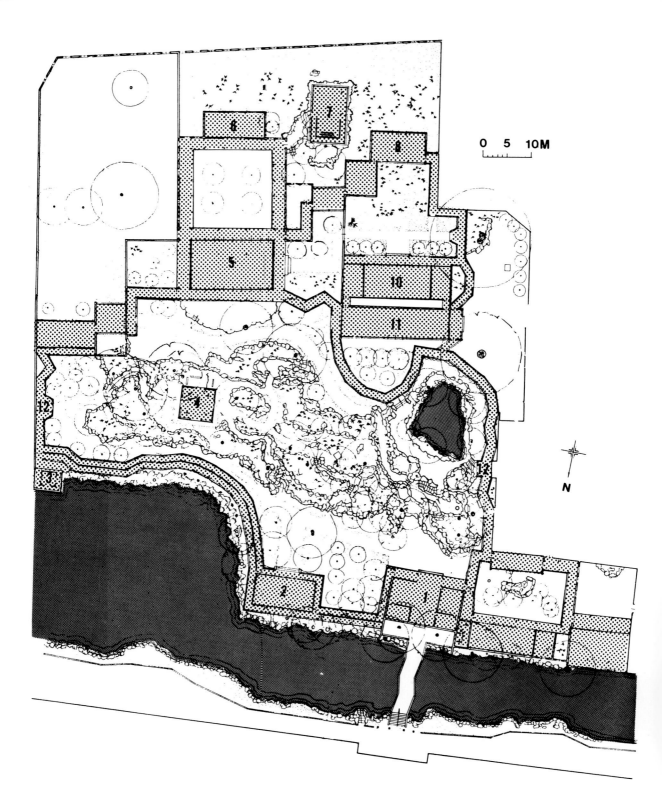

0 5 10M

N

PLAN 5   *Canglang Ting,*
         the Surging-Wave
         Pavilion (Suzhou)

 1. Gate Hall
 2. Waterside Pavilion
 3. Fish-Watching Place, pavilion
 4. Surging-Wave Pavilion
 5. Realizing-the-Truth Hall
 6. Land of Jade Blossom
 7. Mountain View Mansion
 8. Exquisite Green, studio
 9. Look Up with Respect Pavilion
10. Memorial Hall for the Five Hundred Renowned Sages
11. Fresh Fragrance Hall
12. Imperial Tablet Pavilion

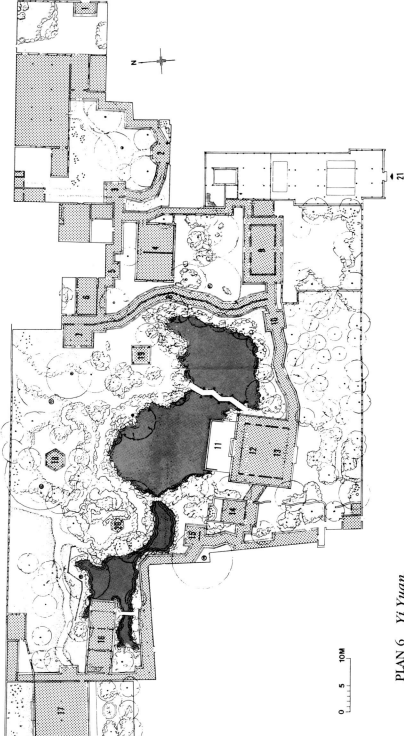

PLAN 6 *Yi Yuan,*
the Pleasure Garden (Suzhou)

1. Entrance
2. Jade-Extending Pavilion
3. Natural and Carefree All Year Round Pavilion
4. Hillside Immortal Music Hall
5. Jade Rainbow Pavilion
6. Stone Boatlike House
7. Locking Up the Green Pavilion
8. Double walking gallery
9. Bowing-to-the-Rock Studio
10. South Snow Pavilion
11. Terrace

12. Lotus Root Fragrance Water Pavilion
13. Hoeing-the-Moon Studio
14. Phoenix in the Parasol Tree, studio
15. Facing-the-Wall Pavilion
16. Pleasure Boat Studio
17. Clear Dew Hall
18. Little Surging Wave, pavilion
19. Golden Millet Pavilion
20. Spiral Hair Bun Pavilion
21. Entrance from the house

0   5   10M

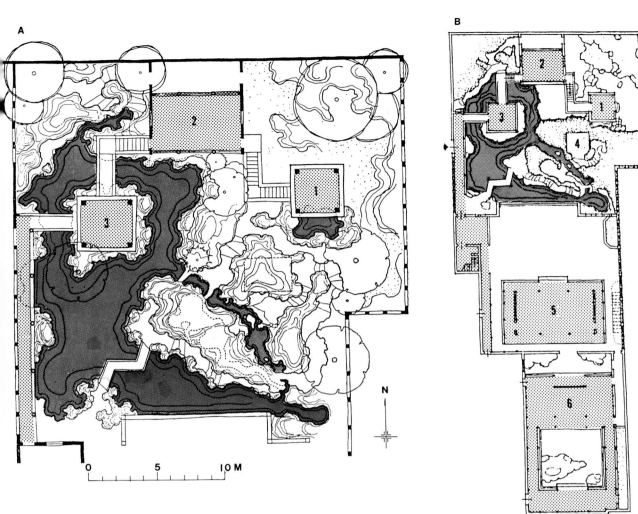

PLAN 7.A   *Huanxiu Shanzhuang,*
            Grace-Surrounding Mountain
            Villa (Suzhou)

PLAN 7.B   *Huanxiu Shanzhuang and the*
            House (Suzhou)

1. A Half Pool of Autumn Water and a Houseful
   of Hill, pavilion
2. Mending-the-Autumn Mountain House
3. Asking-the-Fountain Pavilion
4. Grace-Surrounding Mountain Villa
5. Grain-Possessing Hall

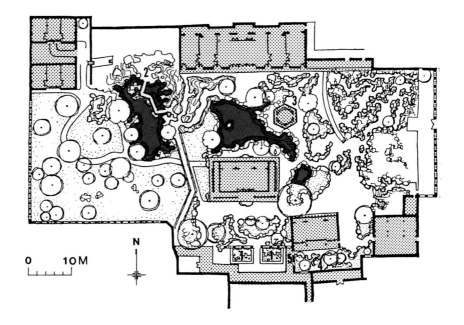

PLAN 8 *Ge Yuan,*
the Bamboo Leaves Garden
or the Isolated Garden (Yangzhou)

1. Spring Hill
2. Summer Hill
3. Autumn Hill
4. Winter Hill
5. Wall openings

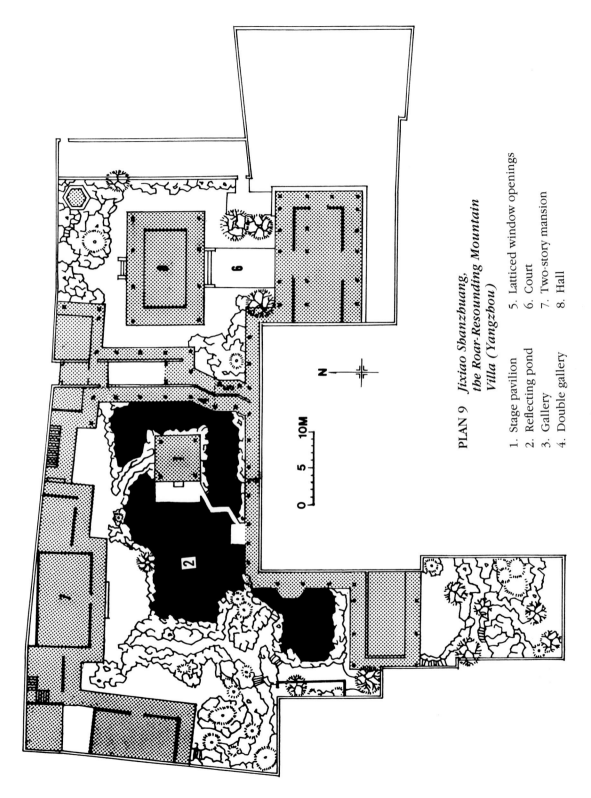

PLAN 9 *Jixiao Shanzhuang,
the Roar-Resounding Mountain
Villa (Yangzbou)*

1. Stage pavilion
2. Reflecting pond
3. Gallery
4. Double gallery
5. Latticed window openings
6. Court
7. Two-story mansion
8. Hall

N

0   5   10M

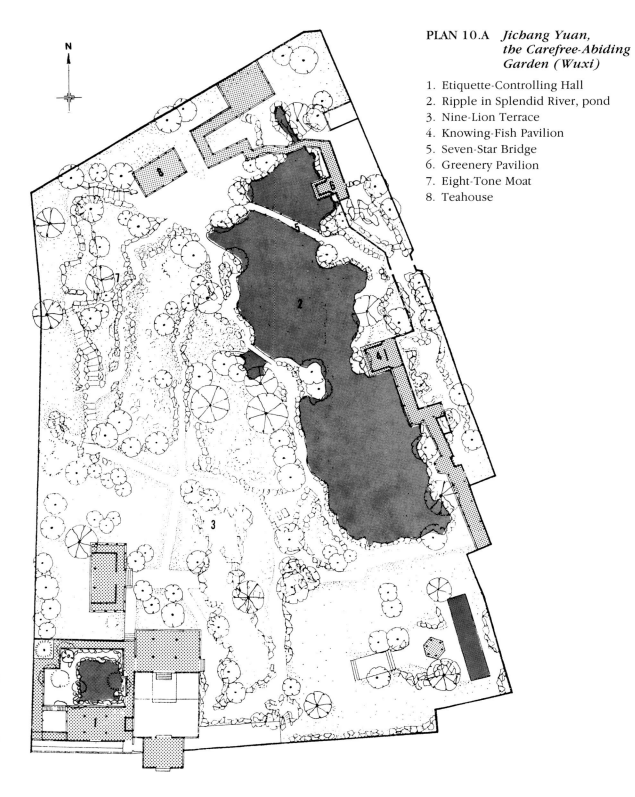

PLAN 10.A *Jichang Yuan,
the Carefree-Abiding
Garden (Wuxi)*

1. Etiquette-Controlling Hall
2. Ripple in Splendid River, pond
3. Nine-Lion Terrace
4. Knowing-Fish Pavilion
5. Seven-Star Bridge
6. Greenery Pavilion
7. Eight-Tone Moat
8. Teahouse

N

PLAN 10.B *Location of Jichang Yuan,*
             the Carefree-Abiding
             Garden (Wuxi)

1. Jichang Yuan
2. Wei Shan
3. Xi Shan
4. Dragon Light Pagoda

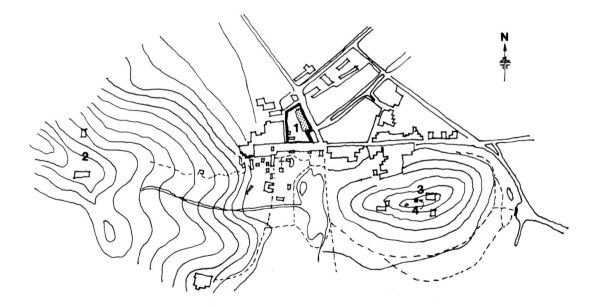

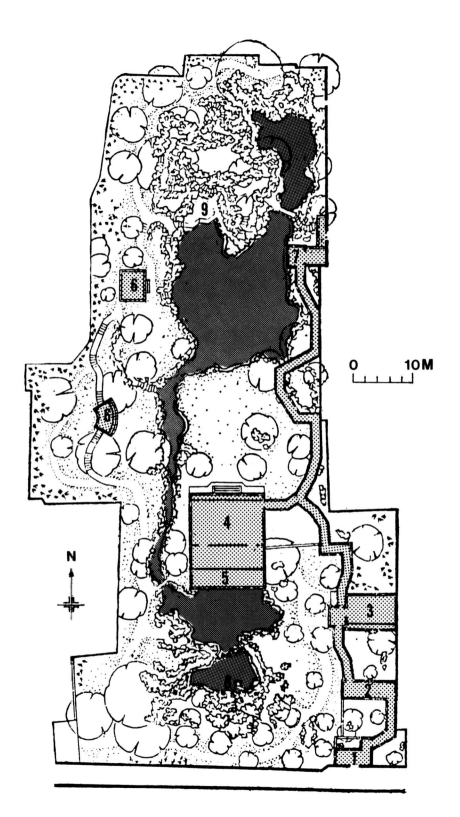

Zhan Yuan,
the Looking-Forward
Garden (Nanking)

1. Entrance
2. Little Studio
3. Flower Basket Hall
4. Wonderful Tranquillity Hall
5. Water Pavilion
6. Pavilion
7. Water Pavilion
8. Waterfall
9. Grotto

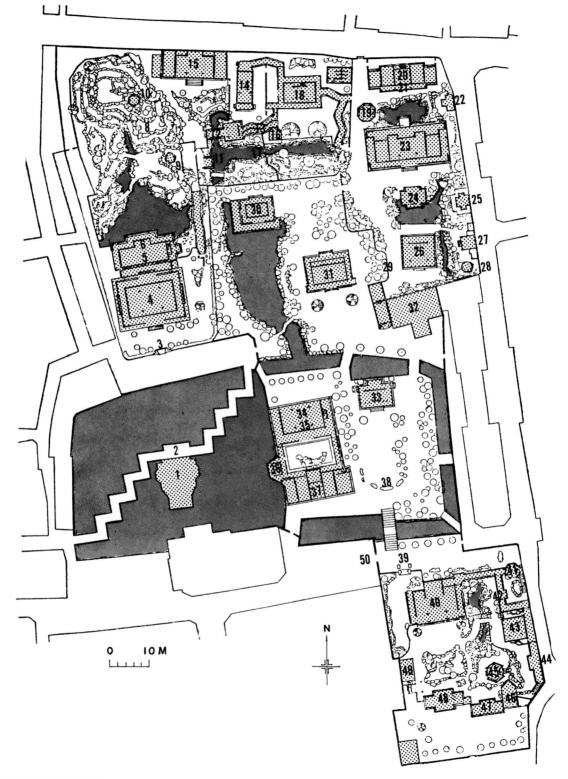

PLAN 12 *Yu Yuan,*
the Pleasing Garden (Shanghai)

1. Lake Center Pavilion, a teahouse
2. Nine-Turning Bridge
3. Entrance
4. Three-Grain-Ear Hall
5. Looking up to the Mountain Hall (ground floor)
6. Rain-Wrapping Attic (first floor)
7. Entering Beautiful Land
8. The Grand Rockery
9. Bowing-to-Beauty Pavilion
10. River View Pavilion
11. Fish Delight Water Pavilion
12. Roofed bridge
13. Double gallery
14. Quasi Boatlike House
15. Assembled Beauty Hall
16. Delight for Both Studio
17. Flower Wall on Water
18. Ten Thousand Flower Mansion
19. Ancient Well Pavilion
20. Treasure House (ground floor)
21. Love's Whisper Chamber (first floor)
22. Nursery for Studying, pavilion
23. Summon Spring Hall
24. Percussion and Singing Stage
25. Tower of Joy
26. Hall of Peace and Brightness
27. Studio of Delightful Tranquillity, pavilion
28. Listen to the Oriole Pavilion
29. Dragon Head Wall
30. Nine Lion Studio
31. Success Mansion
32. Temple of the Supreme Immortal
33. Jade Blossom Hall
34. Reaching-the-Moon Mansion (first floor)
35. Hall of Literary Elegance (ground floor)
36. Tiptoe and Weave Pavilion
37. Green Willows Water Pavilion for Spring
38. Exquisite Jade, rockery
39. Entrance to Inner Garden
40. Static Viewing, hall
41. Phoenix Pavilion
42. Cave Paradise and Land of Happiness
43. Satisfactory Den
44. Another World, gate
45. Towering-Green Pavilion
46. Boatlike House
47. Extending-Purity Mansion
48. Returning-Cloud Mansion
49. Wave-Viewing Mansion
50. Exit

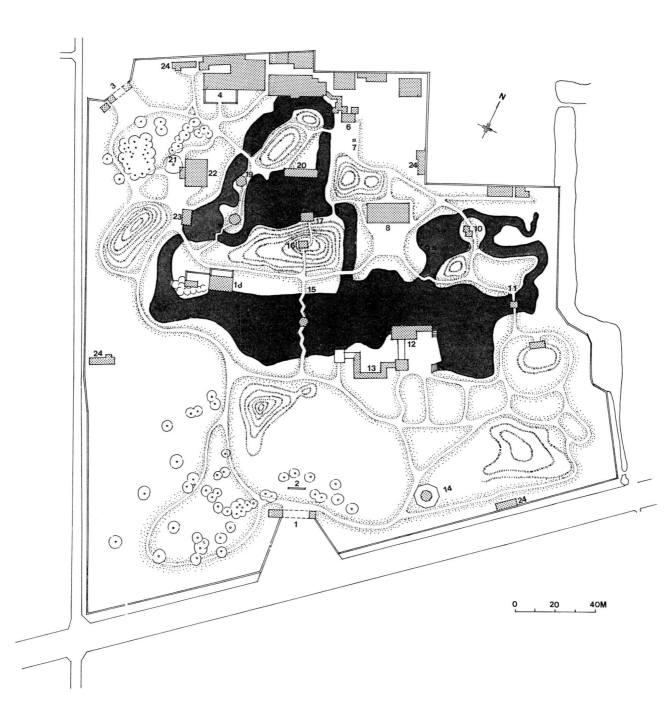

PLAN 13 *Guyi Yuan,*
the Ancient Magnificent
Garden (Shanghai)

1. South Gate
2. Screen Wall
3. North Gate
4. Restaurant
5. Painting the Moon, pavilion
6. Feeble Sound Tower
7. Tang Scriptures Pillar
8. Plum Blossoms Hall
9. Universal Harmony Tower
10. Crane Longevity Studio
11. Willow-Shaded Bridge, pavilion
12. Teahouse
13. Fragrant Crooked Gallery
14. South Pavilion
15. Nine-Turning Bridge
16. One-Corner-Missing Pavilion
17. Floating Bamboo Tower
18. South Hall
19. White Crane Pavilion
20. Unfastened Boat
21. Ancient Chinese Scholar Tree
22. Reclusive Hall
23. Flying-Kites and Jumping-Fish Studio
24. Rest rooms

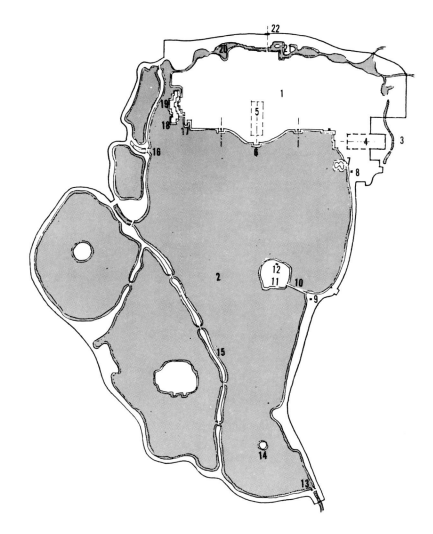

PLAN 14.A *Master Plan of Yihe Yuan,*
the Summer Palace (Beijing)

 1. Longevity Hall
 2. Kunming Lake
 3. Entrance
 4. Imperial court section
 5. Dominant architecture cluster, Buddhist Fragrance
    Tower and Cloud-Dispelling Hall
 6. Cloud-Abraded Jade World, *pailou,* a three-bay arch
 7. Spring-Appreciating Pavilion
 8. Culture God's Tower
 9. Bronze ox
10. Seventeen-Arch Bridge
11. South Lake Island

12. Dragon King Temple
13. Ripple Embroidery Bridge
14. Phoenix Knoll
15. West Causeway
16. Jade Girdle Bridge
17. Marble boat
18. Five Saints Temple
19. Imperial boat houses
20. Back lake
21. Suzhou street
22. North palace gate

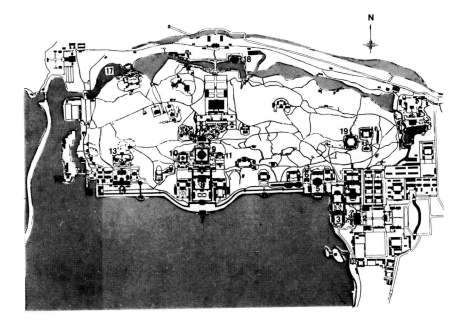

PLAN 14.B   *Architectural Layout of Wanshou Shan, the Longevity Hill (in the Summer Palace, Beijing)*

1. East palace gate
2. Benevolence-Longevity Hall
3. Jade-Ripple Hall
4. Grand Stage
5. Happiness-Longevity Hall
6. Promote Benevolence, inner garden
7. Cloud-Abraded Jade World, pailou
8. Dispelling-Cloud Hall
9. Buddhist-Fragrance Tower
10. Bronze Pavilion
11. Reincarnation Cycle Depository, storage for Buddhist scriptures and relics
12. Wisdom Sea, known as the Beamless Hall
13. Roving in the Painting, inner garden
14. Listening-to-Orioles Hall
15. Marble boat
16. Five-Saints Temple
17. Back Lake
18. Suzhou street
19. Blessing-in-Perspective Tower
20. Garden of Harmonious Interest

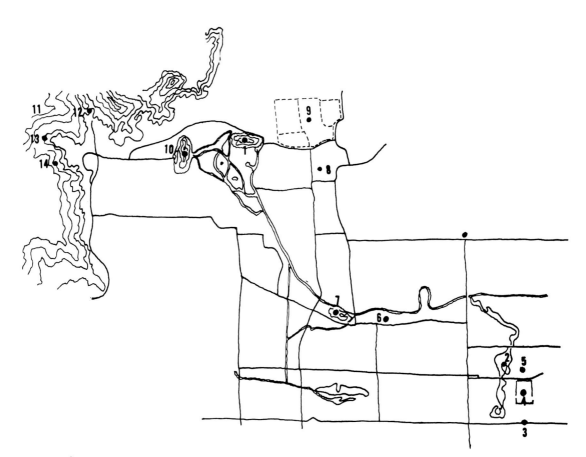

PLAN 14.C *Locations of Yihe Yuan, the Summer Palace;*
Beihai, Gongyuan, the North Sea Park;
and Yuanming Yuan, Garden of Perfect Brightness
(Beijing)

1. Yihe Yuan, the Summer Palace
2. Beihai Park
3. Tianan Men, the Gate of Heavenly Peace
4. The Imperial Palace, known as the "Forbidden City," the Palace Museum at present
5. The Viewing Hill
6. Beijing Zoo
7. The Purple Bamboo Garden
8. Beijing University
9. Garden of Perfect Brightness
10. Jade Fountain Hill
11. The West Hill
12. Lying Buddha Temple
13. Jade Cloud Temple
14. The Fragrant Hill

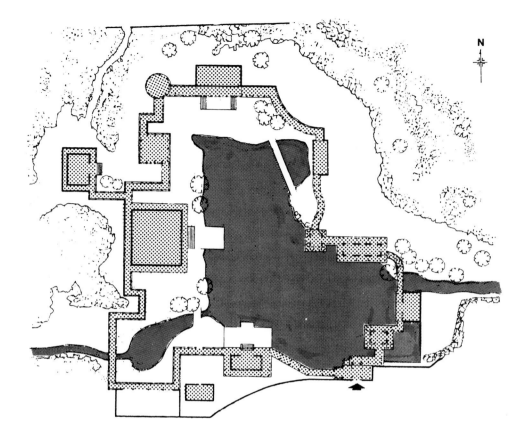

PLAN 14.D *Xiequ Yuan,
the Garden of Harmonious
Interest (in the Summer
Palace, Beijing)*

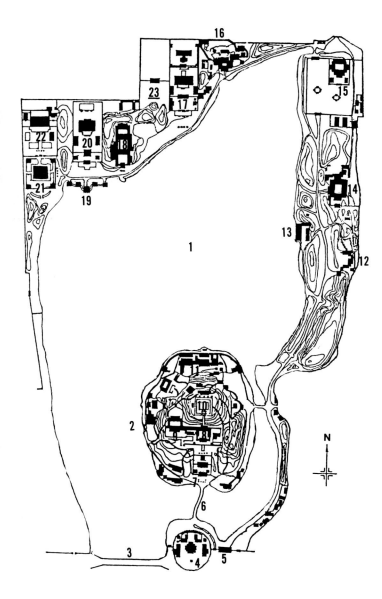

PLAN 15.A *Beihai Gongyuan,*
the North Sea Park (Beijing)

1. Beihai, the North Sea
2. Qiong Dao, Jade Flower Isle
3. Bridge
4. Round City
5. Entrance
6. Eternal Peace Bridge
7. Eternal Peace Temple
8. Straight-Consciousness Hall
9. Heart-Pleasing Hall
10. White Dagoba
11. Ripple Hall
12. House Between Moats
13. Boat House
14. Pleasure-Boat Studio
15. Silkworm Altar
16. Studio of Mental Peace
17. Small Western Paradise
18. Bathing-in-Orchids Studio
19. Five Dragon Pavilions
20. Blessing-Expounding Temple
21. Land of Extreme Happiness, Pure Land
22. Grand Western Paradise
23. Nine Dragons Wall

PLAN 15.B *Jingxin Zhai,*
Studio of Mental Peace
(in Beihai Park, Beijing)

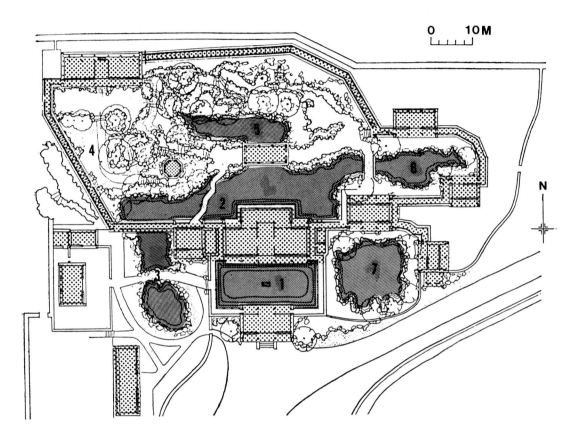

0　　10M

N

PLANS OF FAMOUS GARDENS　*221*

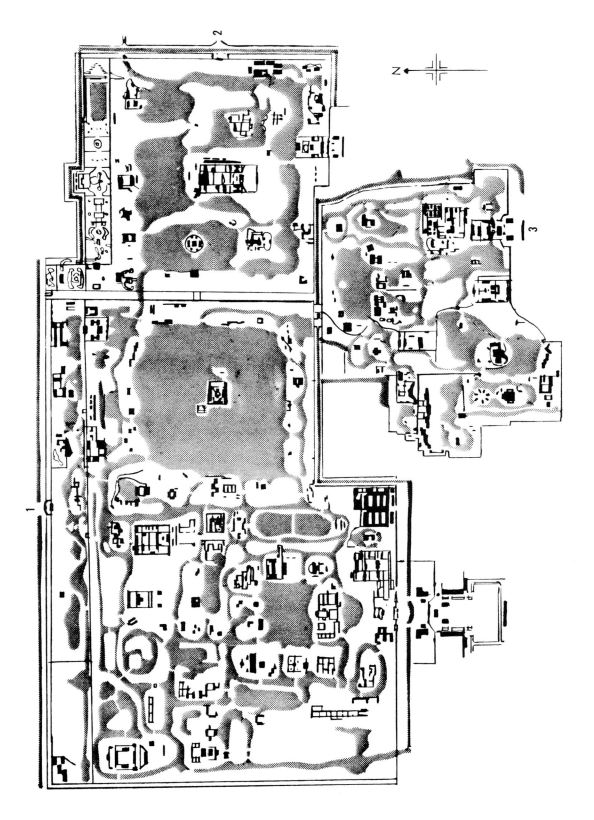

PLAN 16 *Yuanming Yuan, the Garden of Perfect Brightness (Beijing)*

1. Garden of Perfect Brightness
2. Garden of Lasting-Spring
3. Garden of Gorgeous Spring

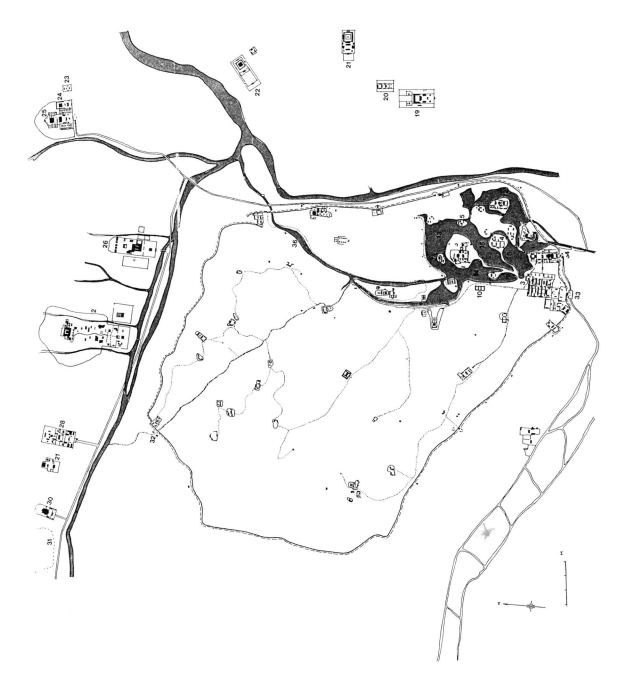

PLAN 17 *Bishu Shanzhuang,*
the Summer-Retreating Mountain
Villa (Chengde, Hebei Province)

1. Resort Palace
2. East Palace
3. Pine Breeze in Ten Thousand Gullies
4. Moonlight over Murmuring River
5. Golden Hill
6. Good Luck Isle
7. Mist and Rain Mansion
8. Avoid Complacency Hall
9. Literary Relish Tower
10. Fragrant Garden House
11. Silver Lake
12. Mirror Lake
13. Clear Lake
14. Good Luck Lake
15. Upper Lake
16. Lower Lake
17. Literary Temple
18. The city of Chengde
19. Universal Benevolence Temple
20. Universal Mercy Temple
21. Universal Happiness Temple
22. Far-Reaching Peace Temple
23. Broad Affinity Temple
24. Blessing All Temple
25. Universal Peace Temple
26. Buddhist Temple of Blessing and Longevity
27. Temple of Buddhist Principle Doctrine
28. Buddha's Image Temple
29. Profound Peace Temple
30. Arhat Hall
31. Lion Garden
32. Northwest Gate
33. Glorious Main Gate
34. Morals Assemblage Gate
35. Literary Garden
36. Crescent Lake

Chronological Table of Chinese Dynasties

DYNASTY	DATE
Shang	1600–1028 B.C.
Zhou	1027–256 B.C.
Spring and Autumn Period	770–476 B.C.
Warring States	475–221 B.C.
Qin	221–206 B.C.
Han	206 B.C.–A.D. 220
Three Kingdoms and Six Dynasties	220–589
Sui	581–618
Tang	618–907
Five Dynasties	907–960
Liao	947–1125
Jin	1115–1234
Song	960–1279
Northern Song	960–1127
Southern Song	1127–1279
Yuan	1271–1368
Ming	1368–1644
Qing	1636–1911

Names of Chinese Gardens – in English and in Chinese

Beihai Gongyuan, 北海公园
the North Sea Park (Beijing)

Beihai, the North Sea 北海
Jade Flower Isle 琼岛
Round City 团城
Eternal Peace Bridge 永安桥
Eternal Peace Temple 永安寺
Straight-Consciousness Hall 正觉殿
Heart-Pleasing Hall 悦心殿
White Dagoba 白塔
Ripple Hall 漪澜堂
House Between Moats 濠濮涧
Pleasure-Boat Studio 画舫斋
Silkworm Altar 蚕坛
Studio of Mental Peace 静心斋
Small Western Paradise 小西天
Bathing-in-Orchids Studio 浴兰轩
Five Dragon Pavilions 五龙亭
Blessing-Expounding Temple 阐福寺
Land of Extreme Happiness 极乐世界
Grand Western Paradise 大西天
Nine Dragons Wall 九龙壁

Bishu Shanzhuang, 避暑山庄
the Summer-Retreating Mountain
Villa (Chengde, Hebei Province)

Resort Palace 行宫
East Palace 东宫
Pine Breeze in Ten Thousand Gullies 万壑松风
Moonlight over Murmuring River 月色江声
Golden Hill 金山
Good Luck Isle 如意洲
Mist and Rain Mansion 烟雨楼
Avoid Complacency Hall 戒得堂
Literary Relish Tower 文津阁
Fragrant Garden House 芳园居
Silver Lake 银湖
Mirror Lake 镜湖
Clear Lake 澄湖
Good Luck Lake 如意湖
Upper Lake 上湖
Lower Lake 下湖
Literary Temple 文庙
The city of Chengde 承德市
Universal Benevolence Temple 溥仁寺
Universal Mercy Temple 溥善寺
Universal Happiness Temple 普乐寺
Far-Reaching Peace Temple 安远寺
Broad Affinity Temple 广缘寺
Blessing All Temple 普佑寺
Universal Peace Temple 普宁寺
Buddhist Temple of Blessing and Longevity 须弥福寿庙
Temple of Buddhist Principle Doctrine 普陀宗乘庙
Buddha's Image Temple 殊像寺
Profound Peace Temple 广安寺
Arhat Hall 罗汉堂
Lion Garden 狮子园
Northwest Gate 西北门
Glorious Main Gate 丽正门
Morals Assemblage Gate 德汇门
Literary Garden 文园
Crescent Lake 半月湖

Canglang Ting, 沧浪亭
the Surging-Wave
Pavilion (Suzhou)

Waterside Pavilion 面水亭
Fish-Watching Place, pavilion 观鱼处
Surging-Wave Pavilion 沧浪亭
Realizing-the-Truth Hall 明道堂
Land of Jade Blossom 瑶华境界
Mountain View Mansion 看山楼
Exquisite Green, studio 翠玲珑
Look Up with Respect Pavilion 仰止亭
Memorial Hall for the Five Hundred Renowned Sages 五百名贤祠
Fresh Fragrance Hall 清香馆
Imperial Tablet Pavilion 御碑亭

Ge Yuan, 个园
the Bamboo Leaves Garden
or the Isolated Garden (Yangzhou)

Guyi Yuan, 古漪园
the Ancient Magnificent
Garden (Shanghai)

Screen Wall 照壁
Painting the Moon, pavilion 绘月
Feeble Sound Tower 微音阁
Tang Scriptures Pillar 唐经幢
Plum Blossoms Hall 梅花厅
Universal Harmony Tower 普同塔
Crane Longevity Studio 鹤寿轩
Willow-Shaded Bridge, pavilion 柳荫桥亭
Fragrant Crooked Gallery 曲香廊
South Pavilion 南亭
Nine-Turning Bridge 九曲桥
One-Corner-Missing Pavilion 缺角亭
Floating Bamboo Tower 浮筠阁
South Hall 南厅
White Crane Pavilion 白鹤亭
Unfastened Boat 不系舟
Ancient Chinese Scholar Tree 古盘槐
Reclusive Hall 逸野堂
Flying-Kites and Jumping-Fish Studio 鸢飞鱼跃轩

Huanxiu Shanzhuang, 环秀山庄
Grace-Surrounding Mountain
Villa (Suzhou)

A Half Pool of Autumn Water and a Houseful of Hill, pavilion　半潭秋水一房山
Mending-the-Autumn Mountain House　补秋山房
Asking-the-Fountain Pavilion　问泉亭
Grace-Surrounding Mountain Villa　环秀山庄
Grain-Possessing Hall　有谷堂

Jichang Yuan, 寄畅园
the Carefree-Abiding
Garden (Wuxi)

Wei Shan　惠山
Xi Shan　锡山
Dragon Light Pagoda　龙光塔
Etiquette-Controlling Hall　秉礼堂
Ripple in Splendid River, pond　锦江漪
Nine-Lion Terrace　九狮台
Knowing-Fish Pavilion　知鱼亭
Seven-Star Bridge　七星桥
Greenery Pavilion　涵碧亭
Eight-Tone Moat　八音涧

Jixiao Shanzhuang, 寄啸山庄
the Roar-Resounding Mountain
Villa (Yangzhou)

Liu Yuan, 留园
the Lingering Garden (Suzhou)

Crisscrossing Ancient Tree Branches Court　古木交柯
Green Shade, water pavilion　绿荫
Bright Zither Mansion　明瑟楼
Greenery Mountain House　涵碧山房
Another World　别有洞天
Lively Region, hall　活泼天地
Pavilion for Free Whistling　舒啸亭
Utmost Joy Pavilion　至乐亭
Osmanthus Fragrance-Smelling Studio　闻木樨香轩
Distant Green Tower　远翠阁
Pavilion for Fine Days, Happy Rains, and Delightful Snow　佳晴喜雨快雪之亭
Crest-Cloud Terrace　冠云台
Crest-Cloud Mansion　冠云楼
Crest-Cloud Pavilion　冠云亭
Crest-Cloud Peak　冠云峰
Emerging-Cloud Peak　岫云峰
Blessing-Cloud Peak　瑞云峰
Cloud-Washing Pond　浣云池
Awaiting-the-Clouds Hut　伫云庵
Respectables of Forests and Fountains Hall　林泉耆硕之馆
Place Returned to Me for Study, studio　还我读书处
Bowing-to-the-Peak Studio　揖峰轩
Viewing in Repose, gallery　静中观
Hut in the Stone Forest　石林小屋
Home of Cranes　鹤所
Five-Peak Immortal Hall　五峰仙馆
Place for Obtaining Rope to Draw from Antiquity　汲古得绠处
Waterside Hall of Fresh Breezes　清风池馆
West Mansion　西楼
Meandering-Stream Mansion　曲溪楼
Moated Pavilion　濠濮亭
Little Immortal Island　小蓬莱
Satisfaction Pavilion　可亭
Another Village　又一村

Master Plan of Yihe Yuan, 颐和园
the Summer Palace (Beijing)

Longevity Hall 万寿山
Kunming Lake 昆明湖
Cloud-Abraded Jade World 云辉玉宇
Spring-Appreciating Pavilion 知春亭
Culture God's Tower 文昌阁
Seventeen-Arch Bridge 十七孔桥
South Lake Island 南湖岛
Dragon King Temple 龙王庙
Ripple Embroidery Bridge 绣漪桥
Phoenix Knoll 凤凰墩
Jade Girdle Bridge 玉带桥
Five Saints Temple 五圣祠
Back lake 后湖
Suzhou street 苏州街
North palace gate 北宫门
East palace gate 东宫门
Benevolence-Longevity Hall 仁寿堂
Jade-Ripple Hall 玉澜堂
Grand Stage 大戏台
Happiness-Longevity Hall 乐寿堂
Promote Benevolence 扬仁风
Cloud-Abraded Jade World 云辉玉宇
Dispelling-Cloud Hall 排云殿
Buddhist-Fragrance Tower 佛香阁
Reincarnation Cycle Depository, 转轮藏
Wisdom Sea, known as the Beamless Hall 智慧海
Roving in the Painting, inner garden 画中游
Listening-to-Orioles Hall 听鹂馆
Blessing-in-Perspective Tower 景福阁
Garden of Harmonious Interest 谐趣园
Tianan Men, the Gate of Heavenly Peace 天安门
Palace Museum, the Imperial Palace, "Forbidden City" 故宫博物馆 紫禁城
Viewing Hill 景山
Purple Bamboo Garden 紫竹园
Yuquan Shan, Jade Fountain Hill 玉泉山
Xi Shan, the West Hill 西山
Wofu Si, Lying Buddha Temple 卧佛寺
Biyun Si, Jade Cloud Temple 碧云寺
Xiang Shan, the Fragrant Hill 香山

Shizi Lin, 狮子林
the Lion Grove (Suzhou)

Ancestral Temple 祠堂
Renowned Hall of Swallows 燕誉堂
Standing-in-Snow Hall 立雪堂
Graceful Bamboo Tower 修竹阁
Imperial Tablet Pavilion 御碑亭
Pavilion for Wen Tianxiang's Tablet 文天祥碑亭
Fan Pavilion 扇子亭
Double Fragrance Immortal Hall 双香仙馆
Tower for Visiting Plum Blossoms 问梅阁
Flying-Waterfall Pavilion 飞瀑亭
Mansion of Faint Fragrance and Scattered Shadows 暗香疏影楼
Stone Boatlike House 石舫
Lake Center Pavilion 湖心亭
True Delight Pavilion 真趣亭
Five Ancient Pines Garden 古五松园
Lotus Hall 荷花厅
Mountain View Mansion 见山楼
Half Pavilion 半亭
Pointing-Cypress Studio 指柏轩
Little Square Hall 小方厅
Lying-Cloud Chamber 卧云室

Wangshi Yuan, 网师园
the Net Master's Garden (Suzhou)

Cloud Ladder Chamber 梯云室
Five-Peak Studio (ground floor) 五峰书屋
Appreciating Paintings Attic (first floor) 读画楼
Void-Collecting Studio 集虚斋
Watching Pines and Appreciating Paintings Studio 看松读画楼
Late Spring Studio 殿春簃
A Branch Beyond the Bamboo Studio 竹外一枝轩
Duck-Shooting Gallery 射鸭廊
Grace-Gathering Mansion 撷秀楼
Sedan Hall 轿厅
Greenery Fountain 涵碧泉
Moon-Arriving and Wind-Coming Pavilion 月到风来亭
Cool Fountain Pavilion 冷泉亭
Water Pavilion for Washing Headgear String 濯缨水阁
Stick to Peace Hall 蹈和馆
Music Chamber 琴室
Small Hill with Osmanthus Groves Studio 小山丛桂轩

Yi Yuan, 怡园
the Pleasure Garden (Suzhou)

Jade-Extending Pavilion 玉延亭
Natural and Carefree All Year Round Pavilion 四时潇洒亭
Hillside Immortal Music Hall 坡仙琴馆
Jade Rainbow Pavilion 玉虹亭
Locking Up the Green Pavilion 锁绿轩
Bowing-to-the-Rock Studio 拜石轩
South Snow Pavilion 南雪亭
Lotus Root Fragrance Water Pavilion 藕香榭
Hoeing-the-Moon Studio 锄月轩
Phoenix in the Parasol Tree, studio 碧梧栖凤
Facing-the-Wall Pavilion 面壁亭
Pleasure Boat Studio 画舫斋
Clear Dew Hall 湛露堂
Little Surging Wave, pavilion 小沧浪
Golden Millet Pavilion 金粟亭
Spiral Hair Bun Pavilion 螺髻亭

Yu Yuan, 豫园
the Pleasing Garden (Shanghai)

Lake Center Pavilion, a teahouse 湖心亭
Nine-Turning Bridge 九曲桥
Three-Grain-Ear Hall 三穗堂
Looking up to the Mountain Hall (ground floor) 仰山堂
Rain-Wrapping Attic (first floor) 卷雨楼
Entering Beautiful Land 渐入佳境
The Grand Rockery 大假山
Bowing-to-Beauty Pavilion 挹秀亭
River View Pavilion 望江亭
Fish Delight Water Pavilion 知鱼榭
Quasi Boatlike House 亦舫
Assembled Beauty Hall 萃秀堂
Delight for Both Studio 两宜轩
Flower Wall on Water 水花墙
Ten Thousand Flower Mansion 万花楼
Ancient Well Pavilion 古井亭
Treasure House (ground floor) 藏宝楼
Love's Whisper Chamber (first floor) 情话室
Nursery for Studying, pavilion 学圃
Summon Spring Hall 点春堂
Percussion and Singing Stage 打唱台
Tower of Joy 快楼

Hall of Peace and Brightness 和煦堂
Studio of Delightful Tranquillity, pavilion 静宜轩
Listen to the Oriole Pavilion 听鹂亭
Dragon Head Wall 龙头墙
Nine Lion Studio 九狮轩
Success Mansion 得意楼
Temple of the Supreme Immortal 老君殿
Jade Blossom Hall 玉华堂
Reaching-the-Moon Mansion (first floor) 得月楼
Hall of Literary Elegance (ground floor) 绮藻堂
Tiptoe and Weave Pavilion 跂织亭
Green Willows Water Pavilion for Spring 绿杨春榭
Exquisite Jade, rockery 玉玲珑
Entrance to Inner Garden 内园入口
Static Viewing, hall 静观
Phoenix Pavilion 凤凰亭
Cave Paradise and Land of Happiness 洞天福地
Satisfactory Den 可以观
Another World, gate 别有天
Towering-Green Pavilion 耸翠亭
Boatlike House 船舫
Extending-Purity Mansion 延清楼
Returning-Cloud Mansion 还云楼
Wave-Viewing Mansion 观涛楼

Yuanming Yuan, 圆明园
the Garden of Perfect
Brightness (Beijing)

Garden of Perfect Brightness 圆明园
Lasting-Spring Garden 长春园
Gorgeous Spring Garden 绮春园

Zhan Yuan, 瞻园
the Looking-Forward
Garden (Nanking)

Little Studio 小轩
Flower Basket Hall 花篮厅
Wonderful Tranquillity Hall 静妙堂

Zhuozheng Yuan, 拙政园
the Unsuccessful Politician's
Garden (Suzhou)

Linger and Listen Tower　留听阁
Pagoda Reflection Pavilion　塔影亭
Floating Green Tower　浮翠阁
Thirty-Six Mandarin Ducks Hall　三十六鸳鸯厅
Leading to a New World, pavilion　别有洞天
Reflection Mansion 倒影楼
Whom I Sit with Studio, pavilion　与堆同坐轩
Dual-Delight Pavilion　宜两亭
Magnolia Hall 玉兰堂
Mountain View Mansion　见山楼
Willow-Shaded Winding Path, walking gallery　柳阴路曲
Fragrant Island, boatlike house　香洲
Truth-Winning Pavilion　得真亭
Pure Will and Far-Reaching Mind, studio　志清意远
Little Surging Wave, enclosed water pavilion　小沧浪
Little Flying Rainbow, roofed bridge　小飞虹
Pines and Breezes Pavilion　松风亭
Lotus Breezes from All Sides Pavilion　四面荷风亭
Leaning Jade Studio 倚玉轩
Distant-Fragrance Hall　远香堂
Fragrant Snow and Azure Sky Pavilion　雪香云蔚亭
North Hill Pavilion　北山亭
Green Ripple Pavilion　绿漪亭
Dwelling Amidst Parasol Trees and Bamboos, pavilion　梧竹幽居
Spring Home of Begonia　海棠春坞
Dainty Hall　玲珑馆
Honored Guest Pavilion　嘉宾亭
Listening to the Rain Studio, pavilion　听雨轩
Embroidery Pavilion　绣绮亭
Leaning to the Rainbow, gate　倚虹
Loquat Garden　枇杷园
Bamboo Hat Pavilion　笠亭

Bibliography

Chambers, William, *A Dissertation on Oriental Gardening,* W. Griffin, London, 1772.

* Chen, Cong-zhou, *On Chinese Gardens,* Tong-ji University Press, Shanghai, 1982.

Gothein, Marie Luise, *A History of Garden Arts,* Vol. 2, Chapters XIV, "China and Japan," and XV, "The English Landscape Garden," J. M. Dent & Sons Ltd., London & Toronto, E. P. Dutton & Co. Ltd., New York, 1928.

Growe, Sylvia, *Garden Design,* Packard Publishing Limited, London, 1981.

* Ji, Cheng (Chi, Cheng), *Yuan Ye, Garden Building* or *Discourse on Gardens,* China, 1631.

Keswick, Maggie, *The Chinese Garden,* Rizzoli International Publications Inc., 1978.

* Liu, Dun-zheng, *Suzhou Classical Gardens,* China Architecture Industry Publishing, Beijing, 1979.

Siren, Osvald, *Gardens of China,* Ronald Press, New York, 1948.

* Tong, Jun, *Essentials of Garden-Building History,* China Architecture Industry Publishing, Beijing, 1983.

* In Chinese.

Index

About the Author

Frances Ya-sing Tsu (Zhu Ya-xin) came to the United States in 1982 as a visiting professor in the College of Architecture at the University of Nebraska. Before that, she taught at Tongji University in Shanghai for nearly 30 years and also practiced architecture. Tsu's multifaceted experience ranges from research and design in furniture, interiors, and architecture to site planning and landscaping. A recognized housing expert in China, Frances Tsu has had extensive design experience in mass housing and in housing standards and prefabrication studies. Her love of traditional gardens and her many opportunities, working as a design professional, to view these scenic spots in different parts of China led her to write this informative guide.*

* Pinyin transliteration of her name, under which she has published.*